A

# TREATISE

ON THE

## SCIENCE OF DEFENCE,

FOR THE

## SWORD, BAYONET, AND PIKE,

IN CLOSE ACTION.

———◆———

BY ANTHONY GORDON, A.M.

CAPTAIN OF INVALIDS, RETIRED.

Quis Martem tunicâ tectum adamantinâ
Digne scripserit?                HOR.

Printed and bound by Antony Rowe Ltd, Eastbourne

TO

FIELD MARSHAL

HIS ROYAL HIGHNESS THE DUKE OF YORK,

COMMANDER IN CHIEF OF THE FORCES,

*&c. &c. &c.*

THIS LITTLE

TREATISE,

CONTAINING THE

SOLID PRINCIPLES

OF

THE SCIENCE OF DEFENCE,

WITH

*SWORD, BAYONET, AND PIKE,*

A SUBJECT, PERHAPS, OF AS MUCH IMPORTANCE, IN ITS
CONSEQUENCES TO POSTERITY, AS ANY ONE
EVER AGITATED IN THIS COUNTRY,

IS,

WITH ALL HUMILITY AND RESPECT,

DEDICATED,

BY HIS ROYAL HIGHNESS'S MOST GRATEFUL

AND DUTIFUL SERVANT,

ANTHONY GORDON, A. M.

CAPTAIN RETIRED.

# CONTENTS.

# DIRECTIONS FOR THE ARRANGEMENT OF THE PLATES.

N. B.—A plate without any number, to face page 19.

# ERRATA.

Page 14, line 20, for "nore" read, " more."

22, for "Sect. 4th," read, " Sect. 5th."

27, line 23, for " deballare," read, " debellare."

45, the word "On guard", is immediately to follow the words "Prepare to charge."

45, line 22, the syllable " ad" should be joined to " vances."

46, for " point," read, " pointe."

47, for " point" read, " pointe."

49, line 30, dele the word " instantly."

# INTRODUCTION.

MAJOR GORDON having been honored by the Commands of His Royal Highness the Commander-in-Chief, through the Adjutant-General, " to turn in his thoughts the subject of " the Science of Defence, and to consider how it might be effec- " tually applied against the cuts of Cavalry ;" and having been also honored by the application of several Noblemen and Gentlemen, requesting information on the principles of the Exercise for Close Action, which he was communicating to a detachment of the Foot Guards ; he has, therefore, the honor of submitting to them, and to the Public, this little Treatise, which attempts to explain those principles, and which is the substance of a Letter on the subject, directed to the Adjutant-General, in obedience to the order.

He is aware of the difficulty of giving an adequate idea of the Elements of this Science, more particularly, as he has been in the habit of demonstrating the powers of the sword by practice, more than by words. He regrets, that his talents are not more commensurate to the subject ; however, such as they are, they shall be willingly exerted in the contribution of this mite of assistance. If, as a Pioneer, he should be found useful in clearing the way, in removing any of those asperities which might retard the progress of our Defenders in their course to glory, he will be highly gratified.

It might be said, that the present strength and glory of the

B

Nation, its Army of eight hundred thousand Heroes, who are resolved to meet and fight, to conquer or die, for their Country, do not require the aid of this Exercise recommended by an Invalid. The Old Soldier rejoices to find that the Nation is now armed, and competent to the demolition of the Enemy.

The exploits of His Majesty's Forces achieved in close action, both by land and sea, have demonstrated their superiority, and are engraved upon the heart of the Country; but as the Discipline is common, and equal, they cannot ensure the destruction of the Enemy without the effusion of patriotic blood at the same time: wherefore that Science cannot be too studiously cultivated, which invigorates individuals with a power of defending themselves, without suffering from the Enemy at the same instant.

This Science renders the destruction of the Enemy inevitable in close action: it inspires unusual confidence; it redoubles the national enthusiasm; it excites a contempt for the Enemy.

Gordon has been flattered as the projector of a new Exercise; but he cannot arrogate to himself the honor of inventing an Exercise, which was practised more than two thousand years ago. His project went only to revive a system which had been neglected for the last sixteen hundred years. On joining the regiment, he was astonished to find no Exercise for close action; no notion of making thrusts, cuts, and parades; no system of defence or offence; for the established Exercises are adapted only to the missile weapon, and to the movements in *Line, Column, Square,* and *Echellon,* &c. Unable to account for this defect, he made much research, first in this country, and afterwards on the Continent, to no purpose. The system every where established was the same, and differed only in some trifling minutiæ. Being thus unexpectedly disappointed, he was obliged to trace the Exercises to their origin. At length, he was gratified with the sight of the Exercise in question, which still remains dormant in the magazines of antiquity; in those magazines which are stored with gold and diamonds, from which great kings, philosophers, orators, poets, and historians, have illumined themselves and their countries.

The established Exercises are descended from the ancient system; in many respects they have been simplified and improved; they are well adapted to the missile weapon; the idle, superfluous ranks are removed, and adjusted in the order established. This order gives them an opportunity of co-operating. The ancients admired facility and simplicity in their movements; they rejected those which were complex and perplexed; such, for example, as " the marching a *square* by its *right*, or by its left, FRONT, " ANGLE, &c." Finding the existing Exercises partly improved in their descent, although much mutilated, and vitiated in the fundamental and essential parts, under these circumstances, and the conviction of his own mind, he solicited the attention of the late General Burgoyne, then commanding the Forces in Ireland, to the project of introducing some kind of Exercise for close action.

The project (in the opinion of the General) was of great magnitude, and required mature deliberation; wherefore, after three months consideration, he thought it incredible that any science could enable one man to defend himself against twenty grenadiers in immediate succession; nor would he believe it, until he had seen the experiment exhibited, and proved by repetition. The General being thus convinced, had no hesitation in ordering a detachment to be trained in the Bayonet Exercise. Unfortunately for this Science, its Protector resigned his situation; but he took care to recommend the prosecution of the subject to the succeeding Commander-in-Chief, Sir William Pitt, who gave it similar encouragement. After repeated experiments exhibited before him and the late Duke of Rutland, who was then the Lord Lieutenant of Ireland, the project was offered, under that illustrious sanction, to His Majesty's notice. His Majesty was pleased to order one hundred recruits to be prepared in the New Exercise: these men were honored by the Royal Inspection, and by His Majesty's high approbation, which was most graciously and directly signified by His Majesty, and after that, also by a royal message delivered by the late Sir William Fawcett, then the Adjutant-General.

From experiments made upon ten different occasions, it appears that this Science doubles the number of the forces in all times and places of close action, and that it invigorates each man with an addition of power twenty times greater than his natural force, as is demonstrated in the Appendix, from the powers of the lever. The present Adjutant-General was also pleased to signify the approbation of His Royal Highness the Commander-in-Chief, with respect to doubling the number, &c. when he honored the detachment of the Foot Guards with his inspection last year.

The discussion of this subject will be in the following order:

1st, Will be noticed the origin of the Science of Defence, and its effect upon the Romans; the attempt of the French to revive it, &c.

2d, The Roman practice founded on mathematical principles; the laws of motion, and the powers of the lever, &c.

3d, The effect of this practice against either Infantry or Cavalry, whether individually or collectively engaged.

4th, Will be subjoined an Appendix, containing a copy of a Letter from General Burgoyne to General Pitt; a sketch of the bones and muscles of the arm, and of its powers as a lever of the third kind, illustrating the subject.

# A
# TREATISE,

*&c. &c.*

---

## SECTION I.

*The Origin and Effect of this Science, &c.*

SELF-DEFENCE is the first law of Nature implanted in all animals; hence men have been impelled to associate, and to frame laws securing the blessings of society. Although men are admirably supplied with passions to excite them to action, with reason to direct their efforts, and with hands to execute; yet they are not furnished with innate ideas, or science, which points out the best mode of using and applying their strength and their hands to any work. If the arts of writing, painting, and the mechanical arts, require skill and dexterity, which result only from time and instruction, the science of Defence, which consists in a just perception of our powers, and in the proper application of our natural strength against the weakest point of the adversary, cannot be the result of inspiration. Our knowledge of this, or any science, is in proportion to our ideas of the principles *.

---

\* These observations are submitted, in reply to the invective which was some time ago published against this Science, by a translator of the late French King's Ordonnance. He prefaces his work by asserting, that any project for instructing soldiers to defend themselves in close action by any specific exercise, must be VISIONARY and CHIMERICAL. But as he confesses that he is a stranger to the science of Defence, not knowing the *fort* from the *foible*, his opinion is so far excusable.

The progress of arms, thus compressed by Horace, viz.

" Unguibus et pugnis, dein fustibus atq ; ita porrò
" Pugnabant armis quæ post fabricaverat usus,"

was, like that of all sciences, by slow gradation. Originating in the East, it migrated to Egypt, whence it was introduced into Greece by Cecrops, as an instrument for polishing his new city, which was, after that, so celebrated as the nursery of arts and sciences under the name of Athens. The Grecian States, however discordant on other points, concurred in the policy of encouraging gymnastic exercises, as is manifest from the signal honors accumulated upon the victors at the Isthmian, Pythian, Nemean, and the celebration of the Olympic games. The conquering heroes *(Olympionicæ)*, were crowned, and rode triumphantly in state chariots, in right lines, through the cities, whose walls were levelled for the purpose, and had their names immortalized in the inimitable effusions of Pindar, &c. The revolution of time was even marked and denominated to do them honor; and hence the period of four years was called an Olympiad.

The Romans, though comparatively illiterate at that time, were superior in the use of the hand weapon, which is thus stated by Vegetius :

" The Romans owed the conquest of the world to their pre-emi-
" nence in the use of the sword, and to a rigid discipline. A handful
" of Romans could have nothing but this science to oppose to the
" multitudes of the Gauls, to the enormous size of the Germans, to
" the number and corporal strength of the Spaniards. We were, at
" all times, inferior to the Africans in the resources of wealth and
" stratagem, and to the Greeks in all arts and sciences; but by an
" unremitting cultivation of the hand weapon, and by a judicious se-
" lection and instruction of recruits in the science of Defence, the Ro-
" mans conquered the world."

This science originated in the custom of sacrificing wretched prisoners of war, supposed to propitiate the manes of heroes slain in battle : thus Achilles gratified himself, and the shade of his friend, with the immolation of twelve captives.

Δωδεκα δὲ Τρώων μεʃαθυμων υἷεας εσθλὰς
Χαλκῶ δηϊόων·

ILIAD, LIB. XXIII. LINEA 175 ;

which is thus elegantly translated by Mr. Pope :

" Then last of all, and, horrible to tell,
" Sad sacrifice ! twelve Trojan captives fell."

Superstition, though tenacious of her rites, yet admitted some innovation in the mode ; she resigned, therefore, the personal exercise of the bloody dagger, and permitted the slaves to exert themselves in slaying one another. Those exhibitions of dexterity and courage attracted multitudes of all descriptions ; in consequence of which, some men of rank, observing the public avidity for these spectacles, erected colleges for the instruction of gladiators in all the minutiæ of the science. These were termed *ludi*, and the masters, *ludimagistri*, or *lanistæ*. Lentulus and Crassus were noted for wealth accumulated by this traffic. There were at least fourteen sects *(familiæ gladiatorum)*, such as the Retiarii, Secutores, Samnites, Galli, Murmillones, &c. &c. In the edileship of Julius Cæsar, he availed himself of that opportunity to gratify the public, by exhibiting three hundred pairs of gladiators in succession. But this science, at first confined to stigmatized gladiators and soldiers, was at length cultivated by all ranks, as an essential branch of a finished education.

Cicero, in his Tusculan Questions, speaking of the grace and magnanimity displayed by the gladiators in their last moments, says :

" Quis mediocris gladiator ingemuit ? Quis unquam vultum mu
" tavit ? Quis non mado stetit, verum etiam decubuit turpiter ?"

" What gladiator of mediocrity has been heard to sigh in the mo

" ment of extremity ? Which of them ever changed countenance ?
" Which of them has not only stood in a graceful attitude, but has
" even fallen with dignity ?"

The ladies also, seeing the effects of this science in adorning the
mind and body, were instructed, decoræ more palæstræ. Hor.

As the use of the sword, in loyal hands, was the bulwark of the
Roman power, so the abuse of it might subvert the constitution, as in
the instances of Sylla and Marius, Cæsar and Pompey, &c. &c.
The gladiator Spartacus, with a handful of similar traitors, proved the
immense advantage he had acquired by this science, by the defeat of
several consular armies ; and if Cicero had not confined the gladiators,
their junction with Cataline must have proved fatal to Rome.

The abuse, and after that, the loss of this science, and of all discipline, concurred in accelerating the fall of the empire.

It does not appear, that from this period until the year 1575, any
effort had been made to recall the science.

About this time, however, under Charles IX. of France, its revival
was attempted ; but as the reformers did not proceed upon mathematical principles, nor on the laws of motion, and the powers of the lever,
it is no wonder that this science should have retrograded, or remained
stationary for such a long interval.

Their views, however, were meritorious ; the existing practice is
derived from them. They exploded the barbarous, empty, insignificant words, *Maindrette, Renverse, Fendante, Estocade, Imbroncade,*
and introduced the significant ordinal terms, viz. PRIME, SECONDE,
TIERCE, QUARTE, QUINTE, and OCTAVE, which are current at this
moment : they have left no names between the QUINTE and the
OCTAVE.

To give authority to the system, their syndics asserted, that it was
the result of experiments from Nature ; that different peasants having
been ordered to make their efforts in succession, concurred in making
their first thrust in PRIME, directing the point high, more to the left
of the antagonist, with their hands in pronation ; that is, with the

*Plate I.*

*Tierce*

*Prime*

*Seconde*

*Quinte*

1

*Quarte over*

*Quarte inside*

*Octave*

2

*R Smirke Jun.r delin*        *Jn.o Lee aqua.*

knuckles and palm downwards, and the convexity of the hand, of course, upwards. See *Prime*, Plate 1st, Diagram 1st.

From this weak position most of the cuts and guards used by cavalry are derived.

The peasants agreed in delivering their second thrust under the arm of the adversary, the hand in pronation. *Seconde*, Diagram the 1st.

Their third impulse was over the adversary's arm, retaining the same position of the hands. *Tierce*, Diagram ditto.

This is an excellent position for cutting vertically downwards.

Being ordered to make a fourth impulse, they rolled their hands into supination, wherein the nails, knuckles, and palm of the hand, are turned upwards. They projected the thrust into the cavity of the arm of the adversary—*Quarte*, the safest and strongest position. Diagram 2d.

They directed the fifth thrust low, under the adversary's arm, with their hand in pronation, and opposed to the right of the adversary. *Quinte*, Diagram 1st. Hence the hanging guard, and the *inside* and *outside* half *hangers*, &c.

The *Octave* is the sixth thrust; the hand is in supination, and opposed to your own right. In quarte, the opposition is to your left.

Such are the simple thrusts, from which all cuts and thrusts, however complex, are derived.

The six simple guards are synonimous with the thrusts, as the guard of quarte, the guard of tierce, &c. &c.

As thrusts are either simple or complex, so are the guards. All cuts are complex motions, or combinations of several simple motions. Notwithstanding this French arrangement of the thrusts, yet it appears from experiments, and the construction of the arm, that the quarte should be placed at the head of all the thrusts and parades, from the strength of the hand in opposing, and retaining the weapon in that position. *Tierce* ranks next to *quarte*; as in *tierce* the hand is over the adversary, and has all the advantages of gravity in striking downwards. The *seconde*, *quinte*, and the *prime* itself, descend from tierce. But these three thrusts, and all guards and thrusts derived from them, such as the *hanging* guard, the *outside* and *inside half hangers*, the *off side* and *near side protects* should be rejected, being dangerous to the persons using them. In like manner should be rejected all cuts, save only two, and all complex thrusts whatsoever; but certain complex parades cannot be too studiously cultivated.

## SECT. II.

*Containing a Sketch of the Roman Practice, which was conformable to Mathematical Principles, to the Laws of Motion, and to the Powers of the Lever, &c.*

PREVIOUSLY to the attempt of explaining the Roman practice, it may not be irrelevant to state what Vegetius says, generally regarding it, in the 11th and 12th chapters of his 1st book. The purport of the 11th chapter is, " that the recruits were exercised twice a day, " every morning and evening, with arms of double the weight of such " as were used in real action : that every soldier and gladiator who had " acquired glory, either in the field, or upon the arena, had been in " the constant habit of exercising, thus heavily armed. That, after " being drilled in the attitudes by a master, and instructed to make the " most forcible cuts, which, according to gravity, are vertical, they were " to practise also by cutting at a post six feet high : that there was a post " appropriated for every soldier : that they were taught how to strike at " the head, sides, and arms; how to advance, by throwing the centre of " gravity dexterously forward upon one leg, and to retire, by throwing " the weight of the body backwards." They were thus critically instructed in a mode of fighting which they did not practice, for the reasons which he states in the 12th chapter, which is transcribed, as a gem of inestimable value, and perhaps the only passage of antiquity which elucidates the Roman practice.

Cap. XII.—" *Non cæsim, sed punctim ferire docendos tirones.*

" Præterea non cæsim, sed punctim ferire discebant. Nam cæsim pug-
" nantes non solum facilé vicêre, sed etiam derisêre Romani. Cœsa enim
" quovis impetu veniat, non frequenter interficit; cum et armis, et ossi-
" bus vitalia defendantur. At contra puncta, duas uncias adacta, mortalis
" est. Necesse est enim, ut vitalia penetret quicquid immergitur.
" Deinde dum cœsa infertur, · brachium dextrum latusque nudatur.
" Puncta autem tecto corpore infertur, et adversarium sauciat ante-
" quam videatur. Ideoque ad dimicandum hoc præcipue genere usos
" esse constat Romanos; duplicis autem ponderis illa cratis et clava
" ideo dabantur, ut cum vera et leviora tiro arma sumpsisset, velut
" graviore pondere liberatus, securior alacriorque pugnaret."

Translation of Chapter the 12th.—" *That the Romans were instructed to strike home with the Point, and not with the Edge of the Sword.*

" Moreover observe, that they learned to strike home with the
" point, not with the edge of the sword, in real action; for the Ro-
" mans not only conquered with facility all those who fought with
" the edge, but also derided such a ridiculous practice; for a cut,
" however forcibly directed, seldom kills, because the vital parts are
" defended both by the opposition of arms and by the bones; whereas,
" on the contrary, a slight prick of the point, penetrating only an
" inch or two into the vitals, is mortal. Again, in drawing the cut,
" the right arm must be raised; consequently this arm, and the right
" side, are *exposed* to *any thrust:* if you deviate, or raise your hand
" out of the line, you are undone; whereas, on the contrary, the
" *thrust* is *sent home,* whilst the body is perfectly *covered* at the same
" instant, and it is sent with such velocity, that the wound is inflicted

" before it is possible to see or avoid it. Such were the incontroverti-
" ble reasons which determined them to use the point, and not the
" edge of the sword, in close action. They were in the habits
" of using such ponderous arms at exercise, for the purpose of
" doubling their dexterity and alacrity with light arms, which they
" used in real action."

The laws of Nature, which measure and determine the moment or force of bodies descending along inclined planes, and compare it with the whole force of gravity with which they fall perpendicularly, are a standard for measuring the force of all cuts whatsoever derived from the laws of gravity.

Gravity is the most obvious phenomenon in all bodies; it pervades the universe. It is that uniform tendency of bodies, exerted in a verti- cal direction to the centre of the earth; it uniformly accelerates all motions, or cuts, vertically downwards, and retards uniformly all bodies projected perpendicularly upwards. The force of any cut from gravity is determined by the following proposition, viz. " The force
" of gravity by which a body descends along an inclined plane, is to the
" whole force of its gravity with which it falls perpendicularly, as the
" height of the plane to its length; or as the sine of the angle of eleva-
" tion to radius."

Plate 2d, Fig. 1st, AC is the plane or cut, BC its base, parallel to the horizon, and AB its perpendicular height, or sine of the angle of elevation. The force of the cut AC is to the force of the cut AB as AB :: AC; that is, as the height to the length of the plane.

The force of gravity of any one cut being thus determined, the force of all are determined by the same rule; for example, fig. 2d, plate 2d, AHN is a circle; ACH is a quadrant containing ten cuts, viz. AC, BC, DC, EC, FC, GC, IC, KC, LC, HC; and there might be ten mil- lions of cuts in the same space, differing in their force from gravity, no two being alike. Their perpendicular altitudes, viz. the dotted lines Bb, Dd, Ee, Ff, Gg, Ii, Kk, Ll, determine their respective forces.

Plate II.

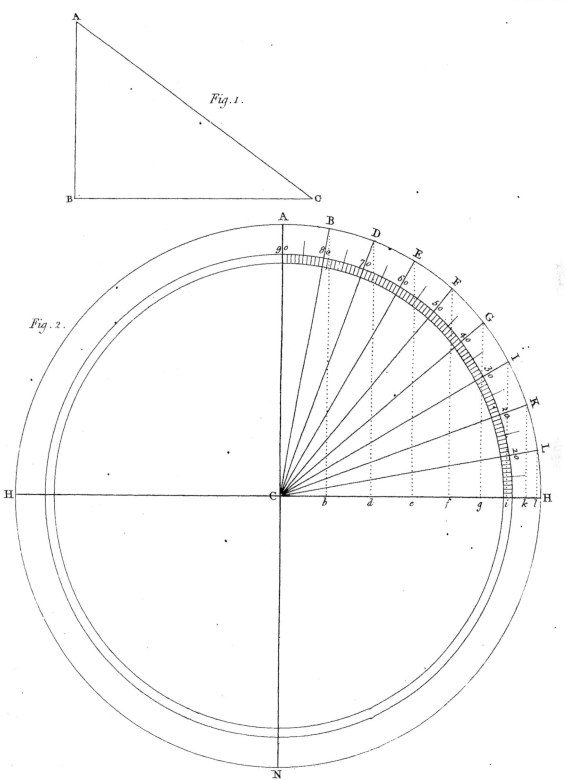

Fig.1.

Fig.2.

J.Le

For example, what is the force, from gravity, of the horizontal cut HC ? Nothing : the horizontal motion is not coincident, but at right angles, with the tendency of gravity, which is vertically downwards.

The force, from gravity, of the cut LC, if compared with HC, is as their altitudes above the horizon : LC, is ten degrees above the horizon, HC is the horizon ; that is, 10 : : 0. By this same rule is determined the force, from gravity, of every other cut, from the horizontal point H, to the vertical point A, where the *sine* terminates in the *whole sine*, radius becoming the perpendicular measuring itself. The vertical cut AC, being impelled by the force of gravity, is the most powerful of all powerful cuts : if compared to any cut ten degrees distant, it is as 90 to 80, &c. &c. ; if compared with the horizontal cut, it is as 90 : : 0. As the force of gravity of all cuts delivered from points above the horizon is precisely as the altitudes of those points, or as the sines of the angles of elevation, so the imbecility of all cuts made from points below the horizon, is in proportion to the depression of those points below the horizon ; all such, therefore, and particularly the cut NC, should be rejected, as they are so diametrically opposite to the laws of gravity, and to the practice of the Romans, as stated by Vegetius, *Q. E. D.*

## SECT. III.

*Representing the Advantages of the simple Thrusts, &c. and the Project
of simplifying and reducing all Cuts and Thrusts to two Denominations,
viz. Quarte and Tierce.*

A SIMPLE thrust is one direct motion, impelled with such celerity as to be finished in the least point of time. A complex thrust is
a combination of two or more simple motions. All cuts are invariably
complex.

Simple cuts are to be used in preference to the complex, as appears
from comparison.

Feints are either single or double, but rarely triple. The single
feint is the least complex of all compound thrusts; it menaces an attack
on one point to cover the real impulse intended upon another. The
French mode (which is erroneous) is as follows : Plate 3d, No. 4, the
point describes the *arc,* or line AB, in the direction of the arrow;
2d, it retrogrades in the same line, say BC, that is, describing the
base, or rather the whole triangle, twice ; 3d, the point is projected
from the point A; that is, the single feint is composed of three motions equal to the three sides of a triangle ; but by Euclid, 20th Prop.
lib. 1, any two sides of a triangle are greater than the third, and the
three are much greater ; and the times being as the space described,
the velocities being equal, the time of the single feint is to that of the
simple thrust 3 :: 1 ; therefore the celerity and advantage of the
simple thrust are in that proportion, *Q. E. D.* Any further illustra-
tion of the advantage of the simple thrust over cuts and thrusts still
more complex than the feint, seems to be superfluous. The right
mode of executing the feint is this : after disengaging from A to B,
from the point B push straight *home,* without returning to A, raising
and opposing your hand, so as to force his blade out of the line ; re-

*Plate III.*

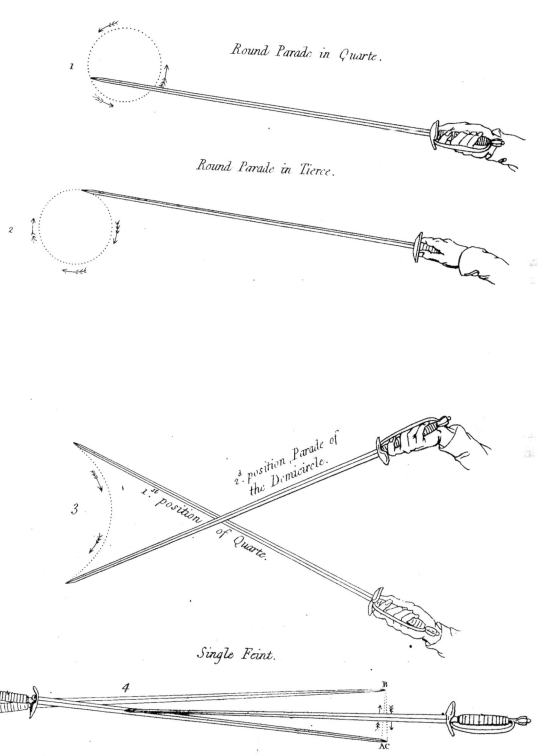

Round Parade in Quarte.

Round Parade in Tierce.

2ᵈ position Parade of the Demicircle.

1ˢᵗ position of Quarte.

Single Feint.

cover quickly, using the round parade of quarte; yet even so, the advantage of the simple thrust would be two to one.

Plate 1st, Diagram 1st. The four simple thrusts, *prime*, *seconde*, *tierce*, and *quinte*, agree in being delivered by the hand in pronation : they are said to differ, because they are directed to different points of the body. The *tierce*, or cut over and outside of the arm, from its superior direction, conspires with gravity in forcing an opening by the dextrous application of the *fort*; but in the *prime*, *seconde*, and *quinte*, there are no such advantages.

The position of the hand is the weakest species of pronation : the fingers opening downwards, are ready to be disarmed by the slightest vertical impulse. The weakness is still greater in the guards derived from these positions : therefore these might be safely reduced to one class, called *tierce*.

The three thrusts, *quarte*, *quarte over the arm*, and the *octave* (Plate 1st, Diagram 2d), are excellent, and agree in the circumstance of being impelled by the hand in the strong position of supination. The arm, wrist, and fingers being turned upwards, the fingers open in that direction, and the impulse which is made upwards against the force of gravity, will generally fail in effecting the disarm : these three differing only in their direction to different points of the body, and in the direction of the opposition of the hand, might therefore be reduced to one class, denominated *quarte*.

It is clear, that an indefinite number of cuts and thrusts may be directed to the various parts of the body; but if all such were to have distinct names, no dictionary could contain them. It is not necessary, for instance, to distinguish every particle of sand by a distinct name, neither would it be subservient to the diffusion of knowledge, which is conveyed in few and general terms; therefore all cuts and thrusts, in the opinion of Gordon, might be reduced to two classes, to facilitate the instruction of His Majesty's brave and illiterate Soldiers, in the event of it being judged proper to give them any idea of the science of Defence in close action.

## SECT. IV.

### The Guards of Quarte, Tierce, &c.

ACCORDING to Cicero's definition of an able swordsman, viz. " vir bonus dicendi (id est) defendendi peritus," worth and merit are the primary qualities, and skill in the science merely secondary.

The defenders of the country, adorned with the inherent primary qualities, will find the science of Defence to be concentrated in the three following particulars, which are mere secondary qualities.

1st, In the graceful command of the body and limbs, and in the acquisition of the particular means which are subservient to this end.

2d, In the possession of the proper line of direction, &c. and,

3dly, In the proper opposition of the hand, and in the application of the *fort* to the *feeble.*

For the purpose of obtaining the first of those essential points, the command of body, you are to be exercised in the three following positions. The first is well known, being the position of a soldier standing on parade : erect, with his heels close, upon a small base. This is a weak attitude, and unfit for defence, &c. ; therefore he is to spring from this into the second position, which is martial, and well adapted to defence and attack. The knees are bent, and the more the better, as the force of the elastic spring will be in proportion to the contraction of the muscles ; the body is balanced on both legs, so that it may rest on both or upon one, and more particularly upon the hinder leg. By this flexibility and command of body, you may be within and out of measure (as it were) at the same moment. Instead of standing square to the front, as in the first position, and presenting the greater diameter of your person, you present your side only, which will be covered by your weapon, and your arm directed in a line before you. The sword is to be grasped by all the fingers, and the thumb

Plate II.

On Guard in Quarte.

Fr. Le qua.

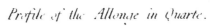

*Profile of the Allonge in Quarte.*

*Plate V.*

1

*Profile of the Extension.*

2

R Smirke Jun.ⁿ delin.

Jn.º Lee aqua.

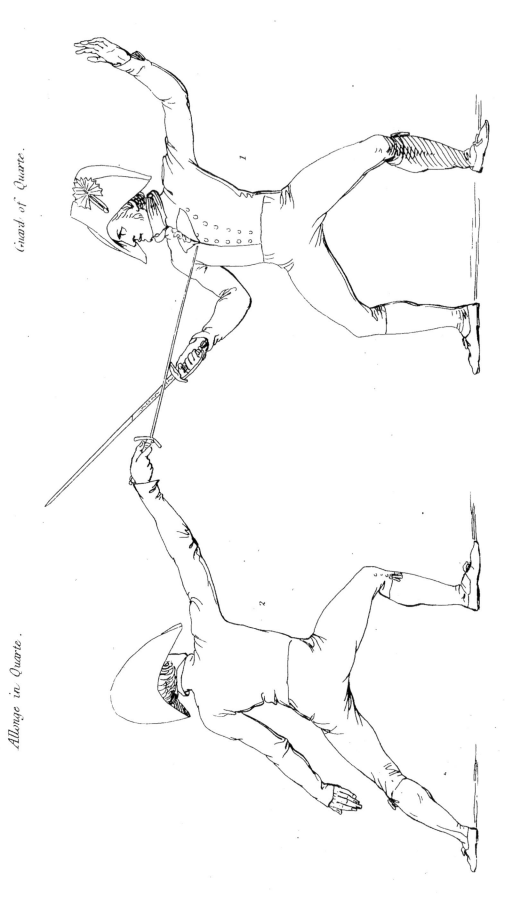

Plate VI.

Guard of Quarte.

Allonge in Quarte.

R. Smirke jun.r delin.

Jn.º Lr. aqua.

extended along the gripe. As the knees are bent, so must the hand be contracted at the elbow. Plate 4th.

This position is termed *on guard*. The sword must not be held parallel to the horizon, as that position would subject your *feeble* to his *fort*, and much less should your point be depressed below the horizon, for the same reason ; therefore it should be raised 30 degrees above the horizon, and directed nearly in the line of his eye. In the second position, you guard or parry *quarte* and *tierce*, and all cuts and thrusts, and advance and retire a few paces, facing your adversary.

Parry *quarte* by your *fort* in *quarte*, and *tierce* by your *fort* in *tierce*. You cannot be too much practised in advancing, retiring, and parrying, simple thrusts and cuts in this attitude. Having fully obtained the command of your person by this practice, and not before, you are to spring from it into your third position, which is that of the allonge. Plates 5th and 6th.

In the second position you sink on your knees, and have all your powers restrained and ready to be exerted : the exertion of these powers will place you in the third position, with your feet about 36 inches asunder at right angles. This attitude is termed the allonge.

The allonge is to be made with all possible rapidity ; this will be better accomplished by engraving the ideas of it upon the mind one after another. Thus, first form your extension: Plate 5th, No. 2; " elevate your right hand in *quarte*, as high as the direction of " your left eye-brow; lower your point in a line of the cavity " under the arm of the adversary ; extend your left hand and left " knee; then project the thrust, rolling your hand still more in " *quarte*, or supination ; throw forward your right foot at the " same instant, 15 or 16 inches, so that your feet may be at least " 36 inches asunder." Plate 6th, Fig. 2d. The foot should resound in striking the ground. Repeat this practice until you can execute it in one rapid motion. Examine your attitude in this third position, and practise unremittingly in the air, until you acquire a graceful precision in the execution. Figure 1st, Plate 6th, gives an idea of guarding the thrust of quarte.

Your own feelings and judgment will best determine the length of your allonge : it should be such as would enable you to recover to your second position with the utmost ease and celerity in real action.

When you are engaged on guard in the second position, the blades are to touch in a point, about ten inches distant from their extremities. The quarte is to be thus delivered :

" Form the extension by a rotatory motion of the arm and wrist
" raised and extended, &c. (Plate 5th, Fig. 2) ; project the sword or fire-
" lock in and along the *identical point of contact*, as in a *nick*; oppose your
" *fort* thus upwards against his *feeble*, as it were in the *nick*. Direct
" your thrust, or cut, in the line, in such a manner as to infix your
" point into the cavity under his arm." See Plate 7th.

All this is to be executed in one motion, and with such celerity as to hit your adversary an instant before your foot strikes the ground. Recover quickly, using your round parade of quarte on this and all occasions.

There are only two good cuts, and these have not been noticed by the French, nor by their disciples : the first is the cut *made vertically downwards* in *quarte*, the second is hurled vertically *downwards* in *tierce*.

Make the vertical cut in quarte thus : " Raise your point vertically,
" and oppose your *identical fort* (that is, that point of your sword
" which is in contact with the shell) to the very extremity of his
" sword; contract your arm ; and having thus secured his *foible*,
" strike in this vertical cut on the quarte, or inside of your adversary ;
" terminate this cut in a thrust, and recover, using your round parade
" of quarte with all celerity." Plate 7th.

In cutting, the hand is to be in the most natural position, between supination and pronation ; but it is to be turned into complete supination when you end your cut in a thrust. The best mode of parrying

Plate VII.

The thrust and cut in Quarte.

The Tierce planted home.

Plate VIII.

1

Pointe Volante in Tierce.

Pointe Volante in Quarte.

2

3

R. Smirke Jun.r delin

Jn.o Lee aqua.

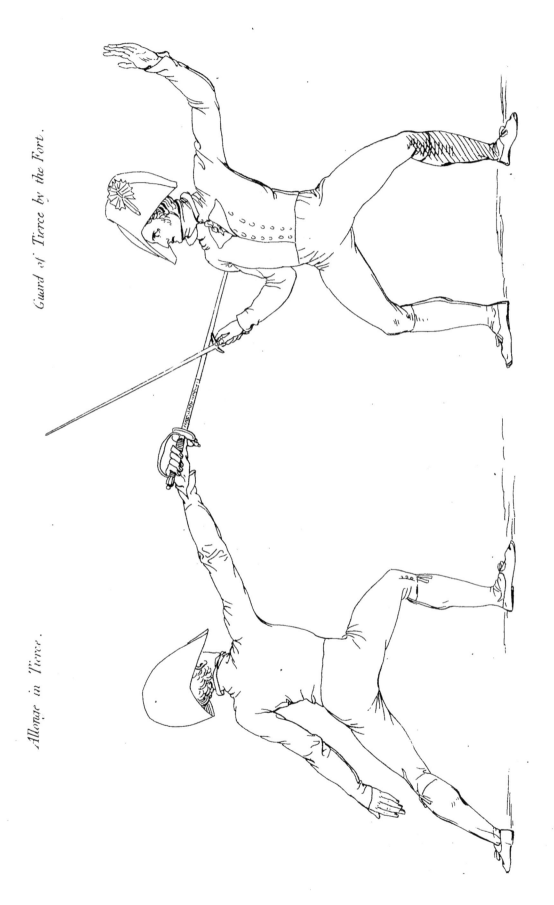

*Guard of Tierce by the Fort.*

*Allonge in Tierce.*

R. Smirke Jun.r delin.

Ja.s Le aqua.

this *cut* is by the *pointe volante*; that is, by contracting the arm, and opposing the fort of the weapon, which must be raised perpendicularly to extricate the foible. By this parade he opposes his fort to your feeble. Plate 8th, Nos. 2 and 3.

The terms *fort* and *foible* are relative, and used to mark the different forces of the different parts of the hand-weapon. That part of the weapon held by the hand is the *fort*; the powers of the other parts of the instrument vary in the following proportion: they are in the reciprocal proportion of their distance from the *fort*; that is, the power of any point decreases as its distance from the fort increases, and *vice versâ*: the reason of which is detailed in the Appendix. The extreme point of the weapon is more weak than any point between the extremity and the *fort*, &c.; the *fort* itself of the instrument is the foible in regard to the power of the elbow, &c. In the application of the fort, and the command of the body, &c. is concentrated the science of Defence.

The guard, cut, and thrust of tierce, are formed by turning the forearm, wrist, and the hand, into pronation. As in the guard of quarte, the hand is to be less in supination than when it finishes the thrust, so in the guard of tierce it is to be less in pronation than when it delivers the thrust.

Besides this motion of pronation, the hand is to describe an *arc* of about eight inches, from the guard of quarte to that of tierce, from the left to the right.

The delivery of the thrust and cut in tierce, is similar in principle to that of quarte, in justly applying your fort. The formation of the extension and the allonge are the same in all thrusts; but your opposition in *tierce*, and in *quarte over* the *arm*, is to your right.

Feel your adversary's blade constantly, but do not press it, as you will be exposed to his time thrust by your relinquishing the point of contact; " therefore, in disengaging from quarte to tierce, move " your point closely, within a hair's breadth of his blade; so quickly, " that your change shall be imperceptible, your hand being in supina-

" tion, as it was before : for if you roll your hand into pronation as
" you change your point, your motion will be wide. Roll your hand
" into pronation as you project the thrust *along* his blade, in the *point*
" *indented* in it, as it were in a *nick*, to direct your course. Oppose
" your hand high, and over his blade, to your right. Direct your
" point into the cavity under his arm." His effort to parry this thrust
(if you have seized his *foible),* by his parade in *tierce,* will materially
serve you, as it will be a *fulcrum* assisting your thrust, unless your
sword whips or bends. Plate 8th, No. 1, gives an idea of planting
the tierce.

Engaged in *quarte,* if you find a direct thrust or cut impracticable
for you to execute, but not otherwise, raise your point vertically ;
apply your *fort* to his point in *tierce,* and cut down vertically and forcibly, ending your cut in a thrust. The best mode of guarding this
thrust, &c. is by the *pointe volante* in *tierce,* thus extricate your
foible by raising your point vertically, with your hand in tierce. By
this mode, his *foible* will come to your *fort.* Plate 8th, No. 2, the
pointe volante.

The *seconde* differs only from *tierce* in its direction, which is under
the arm ; it is generally returned after you have parried the *quarte*
*over,* or the *tierce.*

The thrust of *prime* is, or may be, returned after the parade in
*prime.*

Although no guard can be weaker than that of *prime,* excepting the
modern guards derived from it, such as the *protects,* &c. yet it is useful in one case, and in that only ; namely, in guarding off a forcible
*quarte* over the *arm* ; for if by his fort he has seized your *foible,* in
pushing his quarte over, you cannot parry this thrust by your parade
of tierce ; on the contrary, your resistance in tierce will serve him as
a fulcrum : for his sword, which was a lever of the third, that is, of
the worst kind, before he had pushed it into its present situation inside
your arm, now becomes a lever of the first, that is, of the best kind ;
therefore, instead of resisting in vain, submit your point, and

Plate IX.

Front View of the Guards.

Prime.          Quarte,     &     Allonge in Quarte.

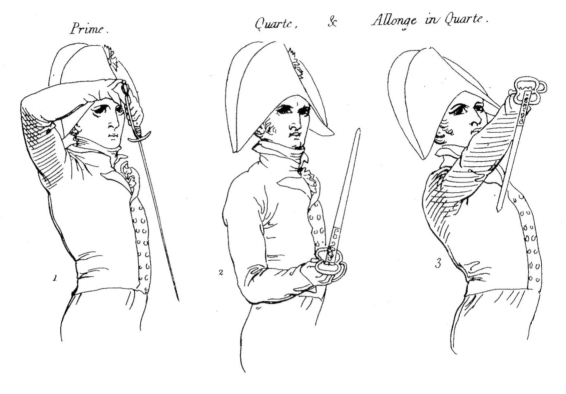

1          2          3

Quinte, or hanging Guard.

4

R Smirke Jun.r delin

Jn.r Lee aqua

contraȼt your hand in *prime*; thus his *foible* will come to your *fort*.

The better mode of parrying is by the *pointe volante* in tierce.

The *quinte* (Plate 9th, No. 4) seems to be unworthy of notice. The quarte over the arm is executed by disengaging your point closely. Spring your fort to his point, and hurl the thrust into the cavity under his arm, turning your hand into complete supination. Your opposition is to your right, as in tierce.

The oȼtave is a good return, direȼted under his arm, after you have parried *quarte* over, or *tierce*. After you parry quarte over, or tierce, return tierce ; if you see no opening for *tierce*, return the *oȼtave*, that is, *quarte under his arm* instead of the *seconde* ; you may, however, slide in tierce, and instantly dart in seconde, which is tierce direȼted under his arm : recover quickly, upon all occasions using your round parade of quarte.

Although the guards of quarte and tierce, and their combinations, are sufficient for individual defence ; and although the general adoption of these guards, &c. would eventually tend to the destruȼtion of the enemy not similarly disciplined ; yet if that moment should unhappily arrive (which may God avert !) when the enemy would also apply the science of Defence to the use of the bayonet : in such event, the parades of quarte and tierce would not answer the purpose of defence as effeȼtually as the guards which are *here* termed the *pointe volante* in quarte, and the *pointe* in tierce (Plate 8th) ; for the parades of *quarte* and *tierce* are too wide to be used by troops in close order. For this reason, the Writer took the liberty of deviating from the practice established in the schools, by introducing the *pointe volante* instead of quarte and tierce.

From all the experiments he has been ordered to make with the men, whom he arranged in an order much closer than any existing, it appears that no man was hurt in the ranks by the wide guard of his comrade standing on the right or left. The parade of the pointe volante produces this desirable effeȼt. Secondly, it is more quickly and easily executed. Thirdly, it gives more facility in opposing the *fort*, and withdrawing the *foible*, in which consists the essence of the science. Fourthly, because the return from this attitude is irresistible : it is impelled vertically downwards by the united force of the muscles ; and this impulse is aided by the accelerating force of gravity in the perpendicular direction ; whereas the force of gravity in favour of *quarte* and *tierce* acts feebly, because diagonally, on an inclined plane. And lastly, because no parade of quarte and tierce, nor combination of these, can parry the return from the *pointe volante :* nothing but the parade of the pointe volante itself can effect it.

## SECT. IV.

### *Respecting compound Thrusts, Cuts, Parades, &c.*

An idea of the simple thrusts, and the project of compressing them, having been previously submitted, in this Section will be offered a sketch of the complex thrusts, &c.

The weakness of the *prime, seconde,* and *quinte,* has been already remarked : if these are radically bad in their simple state, all modifications and combinations of them, in *feints,* glissades, circles, and round parades, are still worse, and therefore should be rejected.

The seconde should not be parried by the *half-circle,* but by a little impulse of your fort in *quarte,* which will probably disarm him. If you throw in the octave at the instant he pushes *seconde,* you will both parry and hit him at the same moment, as his *foible* will come against your *fort* ; but your round parade of quarte will break all such returns. Parry his quarte over with your round parade of quarte, and return quarte, or quarte over, or a vertical cut, which, if he parries, dart in *quarte under* his arm as you are in the act of recovering.

The glissade is a sliding movement along his blade, intended to draw him from the line, and to expose him to a thrust or cut. The glissade is dangerous, as he may hit you on the first movement by his simple thrust, having two to one in his favour. The glissades in simple quarte and tierce are dangerous, but the glissades of *seconde*, *prime*, and *quinte*, are still more useless.

The *flanconnade* is a thrust directed to the lateral part of the belly : make use of it as a return from your round parade of quarte, by pressing down his point with your *fort*; the resistance of his point will assist the direction of your *flanconnade*. If he submits his point to your force, and comes to the second position in quarte, your *foible* will come to his *fort*; that is, he will parry, and perhaps hit you, in quarte. The mode of executing these little thrusts, &c. will be better illustrated by the example and living voice of a master, than by this detail.

Notwithstanding the danger generally resulting from the use of all cuts, and compound thrusts, and more particularly from any combinations of the guards of *prime*, *seconde*, &c.; yet the complex guards, termed the round parades of *quarte*, of *tierce*, and of the half circle, cannot be sufficiently practised. These guards counteract and confound the projects of the adversary. The round parade of quarte circled twice round with celerity, and combined with the half circle annexed; or the rapid rotation twice, or thrice, of the half circle, with the round parade immediately annexed, or any combination of the round parade of quarte with the round parade of tierce, terminated by simple quarte and tierce, form a *shield* sufficient to guard off all cuts and thrusts whatsoever.

Plate 3d, No. 1. The round parade in quarte is thus formed :

" With the point of your sword or bayonet describe the circle in the
" direction of the arrow (which circle is the base of the conical surface
" described by your weapon); feel his blade, by adhering to the point

" of contact as you circle ; protrude his blade with dexterity, so as to
" bring it round to your former position of quarte ; finish your parade
" with a degree of energy." If he circles twice, or oftener, repeat
this parade, immediately annexing the half circle, whereby you will
cross his sword, and perhaps disarm him ; or you may annex to this
parade your round parade of tierce, which will either disarm or drive him
from the line. Dexterity, in the combination of these parades, will
enable you, although blindfolded, to parry all superior cuts and
thrusts.

No. 2, Plate 3. The round parade of tierce is thus formed :
" With the point describe a circle in the direction of the arrow, from
" your right towards your left ; adhere closely, as if the swords were
" tied in the point of contact ; finish this circle with a degree of force,
" in or near to the point of its commencement." If he circles, repeat
this parade, and unite to it the round parade of quarte, or simple
quarte and tierce. The *tierce*, the *quarte over*, the *quarte under* the
*arm*, and the *vertical cut*, hurled down along his blade, are all excellent returns immediately after this parade.

The half-circle (Plate 3d) is formed thus : " By a rapid twirl of your
" hand, with your point describe the segment or arc of the circle in
" the direction of the arrow. The point is depressed, and the hand
" raised as high as your left eye-brow. Take care that in all parades
" whatever, you bend, and do not extend, your right arm." This will
be accounted for in the Appendix, where the errors of the established
practice are pointed out. The repetition of this parade forms circles ;
it collects all thrusts and low cuts ; and when combined with the octave,
it is a complete shield for defence, if he feigns parry with the half-
circle ; unless you choose to time him, or to break all his projects
with your round parade of quarte. If he deceive your *half-circle*, only
extend your hand in *octave*, and he must fall on your point, &c.

Plate X.

Giving point.

Near Side protect.

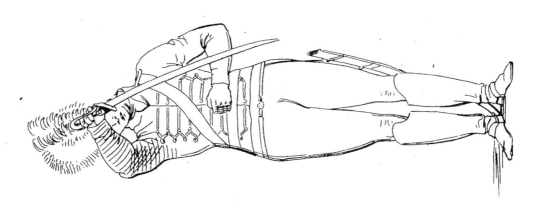

### DISARMING.

The dexterous combination of the round parades will enable you frequently to disarm your adversary. The weakness of the hand in pronation, particularly in the thrusts, cuts, and guards of *prime, seconde,* and *quinte,* is evident. This weakness is still more manifest, in the guards termed the *hanging* guard, the *protects,* and the inside and outside half-hangers, &c. &c. See Plates the 9th and 10th. No aid from the sword-knot can prevent the fingers from opening and yielding to any impulse in the vertical direction, when the sword is held in these positions. But even a tolerable swordsman may be disarmed in the following circumstances: 1. If he changes from tierce to push quarte, " cross his foible from your left towards your right, in the direction " of the opening of his fingers, direct your point in the line towards " his right eye, allonge, and you will both *hit* and *disarm* him."

2. If he cuts over your point, or pushes *quarte-over,* " use your " round parade of quarte; instantly rolling your hand into pronation, " direct your point in the line as before.

3. " Parry any assault made over your arm with the *pointe volante* " in tierce, hurl down the vertical cut, end it in a thrust, opposing " your hand well in quarte," and he will be *cut, hit,* and *disarmed.* This return from a firelock is irresistible.

4. If he pushes *prime, seconde,* or *quinte,* &c. his hand is ready prepared to be disarmed by the slightest impulse of your weapon in quarte, touching his foible. Be careful to disarm in the line, that you may not be exposed, in the event of your not succeeding in your plan.

5. If he pushes or cuts under your arm, " rotate your hand, describing " the *half-circle* three or four times in continuation; adhere closely " to his blade, and he may be thus disarmed." Your point, in this case, describes circles, although this guard is termed the *half-circle.*

6. The following mode of disarming is safe and certain, however unfair it might be deemed in the schools: " Parry his quarte over with

E

" your round parade of quarte, and before his foot strikes the ground,
" depress his *foible*, and adhere to it with your fort ; seize the fort of
" his sword with your left hand, and he will be instantly disarmed,"
&c. &c.    Attempt none of these modes of disarming before you feel
yourself completely dexterous in the preceding parts.

## OF THE TIME-THRUST.

Timing is the summit and very last stage of the science of Defence,
and not to be attempted, except by the ablest swordsman.    It consists
in the anticipation of your adversary, by *nicking* that *point* of time
which is the most favourable and safe for you to make a thrust.    The
thrust delivered at this critical moment, is called the time-thrust, and
is of four kinds.

The first is, the time-thrust, which you deliver on his first movement
to assault you, when you are both engaged within the proper measure.
As, suppose he raises his point, or feigns ; in either case, dart in a
simple thrust, opposing your fort, either in quarte or tierce, as the
case may require, and you will probably anticipate him, it being above
two to one in your favour if you *nick* the time.

2. The *time* of the *arrest* is a decisive thrust, when properly executed.    Be careful to take your station on guard, at least, twenty-four
inches beyond the extent of his allonge ; at this distance he cannot
reach you ; he must therefore advance one step.    He means, suppose,
to engage your blade in tierce, " do not meet or touch his blade with
" yours, but *nick* the time of his first movement, and anticipate him
" by your well-delivered *quarte*.   Recover quickly, and spring back
" to your former ground, or rather twenty-four inches farther back.
" Use your round parade of either quarte or tierce, as you are recover-
" ing" ; repeat the same, if you can seize an opportunity, as it will
be safer for you to act in this manner, than to risk a contest with him
in close action.    You give the time-thrust gratis, unless he is pre-
eminent in the art.

3. Should he, standing out of measure as before, advance to join

your blade in *quarte,* " do not suffer your blade to be touched, *seize*
" the *time* of his advance, and send *home* a quarte over the arm.
" Spring back to your guard as before; you may throw in a *quarte*
" under his arm as you recover."

4. *Counter-timing.* If your antagonist should decline to advance,
in the expectation of timing you as you advance, you may counter-
time him, in this manner : " Advance in tierce, to excite him to de-
" liver his time-thrust in quarte; as you are advancing whirl your
" hand forcibly into the *half-circle,* with your point directed in the
" line, and you will parry and counter-time him at the instant he
" delivers his thrust."

Again, suppose he will not advance, but rather wait, for the purpose
of timing you on your first movement. He stands guarded in tierce
to allure you to engage his blade in *quarte,* that he may *time* you with
his *quarte-over,* " as you advance form the *pointe volante* in tierce,
" and his foible will be precisely applied to your fort; from this po-
" sition hurl down a vertical cut; end your cut in a thrust along his
" blade, over his arm." If you succeed in this stroke, as you must
if you do your duty, you may continue to pour in thrust after thrust
incessantly until he submits. For you are to carry in your mind the
memento of Virgil, as particularly applicable to your art :

" (Hæ tibi erunt artes) pacisque imponere morem ;
" Parcere subjectis, et debellare superbos."

Which is thus elegantly rendered by Mr. Dryden :

" To tame the proud, the fetter'd slave to free ;
" These are imperial arts, and worthy thee."

If, however, your antagonist hath recovered quickly, and parried
your assault by the *pointe volante,* which seems to be the only parade
adequate to the purpose, the assault may be continued. In this case,
the best general rule is to use your round parades, and the pointe volante. Hesitate not to excite him to cut at your lower extremities.

For example, if he cuts low at your thigh, withdraw it a little; seize this critical moment and cut down vertically through his face; terminate this cut in a thrust, in conformity to the Roman practice, as in Plate 11th.

---

## SECT. VI.

*A cursory View of the Origin and Defect of the established Exercises.*

READER, in the preceding Sections you have a sketch of these elements, the cultivation of which rendered the Romans invincible in close action. Should you perceive symptoms of languor in either the Writer or in yourself, from too close attention to rigid principles, you are recommended to lay down this Treatise, and vary the scene. Take up your sword or firelock, and refresh yourself with exercise. Examine and adjust your attitudes before a glass. The practice of allonging first in the open air, and after that against a post, will contribute to invigorate your limbs, and to grace your person. You had better avoid the diversion of *running* at a *post*, to take the ring on the point of your sword; such ludicrous practice tends only to ruin your *opposition*, and consequently to expose your person.

As you may be speedily tired with the severity of this sword exercise, relax yourself, by marching according to the rules prescribed by the established regulations. Your stile and energy in marching will be marked with uncommon ease and precision. This must be the consequence of your previous practice in the positions, which are calculated to produce the graceful command of your person and limbs. Being now sufficiently refreshed, and practised in the elements of the science, you are no doubt desirous to see the means of their practical application against either infantry or cavalry, whether individually or,

Plate XI.

"Nam cæsim pugnantes non solum facile vixere, sed etiam derisere Romani. Veg."

collectively engaged. The Writer equally wishes to come to this main point; but as he is at this moment a little fatigued, he proposes a little excursion, and he will think himself much honored by your company on the occasion. It cannot be unpleasant to review some small portion of those flowery fields which are sown with golden grain. If it be a deviation, it will not be unprofitable, to pay a short visit to the Father of the established exercises. You will be sure to find him always at home, and like the divinity diffused over every part of those princely domains, he hath bequeathed to posterity,

Spiritus intus alit, totamque infusa per artus
Mens agitat molem, et magno se corpore miscet.
ENEID V.I.

———————— one common soul
Inspires, and feeds, and animates the whole.
This active mind infus'd through all the space;
Unites and mingles with the mighty mass.
DRYDEN.

Posterity cannot be sufficiently grateful to Pisistratus! The divine works of Homer were either neglected or sung in detached fragments, to the reproach of the period of 350 years after their composition; his royal genius arranged them in the order you now read them. This, with innumerable similar circumstances, proves the tardiness of the human mind in improvement, and its delight at the same time in holding fast the truth, the moment it obtains a fair view of it.

Instead of deviating, this little excursion will conduct you in the most direct road to the science which will end your journey. It will shew you the defect, the existence and nature of the malady : and this will be a considerable step towards the remedy.

Every line in Homer is a clear demonstration of the beauty and benefits of discipline, of the modes of forming, organizing, and of moving armies in either line or column, &c. &c. He delineates the general principles which are applicable according to the various circumstances of war : common justice to a subject of such magnitude would require volumes. But here you are limited to the cursory glance at a passage or two selected from what is indefinite. You see Homer every where, even in the detail of minutiæ. For example :

Previously to the royal inspection, which he exhibits for your information in all similar cases, he has presented you with the most beautiful and complete return of the strength of the fleet and of the forces. He has not only furnished the precise numbers in each corps, but also the proper names of their officers ; he most accurately delineates their respective countries, towns, and cities, and also the trade, agriculture, and manufactures, in which each of these was then most conspicuous. These harsh and rugged materials, which must have been intractable in any other hands, are polished down and compressed in his harmonious return. Besides, you see the rank, merits, and characters, of the officers and of their men so strongly depicted, that it is impossible for his Majesty to err in his choice ; with a glance, he can select that particular officer and corps the most completely qualified for the performance of any particular duty. He now has his army in his hand, and can dispose it to the utmost advantage.

Are any modern returns comparable to that of Homer, either in beauty, accuracy, or in the magnitude and importance of the information contained ? Can you with such a model before your eyes, find it difficult to make a return of the strength of a few battalions ? and to observe " whether or not their formation is according to order, " the proper distances in column and *echellon* are preserved, the wheel- " ings just, the formations into line true," &c. &c. &c.; but unluckily, he has left no return of the accurate mode of engaging and of fighting your troops in close action ; no mode of defence or offence ; no mode of making accurate thrusts, cuts, and parades ; and as you have no practice of that kind, you can have no returns. Your returns and observations must be confined to the movements, which are only preliminary steps, subservient to the action; but these go no farther, they enter not into the science of Attack or Defence; they cease, unluckily, in the crisis of action; the crisis which calls the loudest for science and dexterity.

Had Homer, the father of the established exercises, existed at this moment, how enraptured must he have felt himself in witnessing that divine enthusiasm which animates every bosom from the one extremity of the empire to the other. Now might he exclaim,

" To count them all demands a thousand tongues,
" A throat of brass, and adamantine lungs."

You see that his stile in marching the phalanges in review before you, in slow and quick time, has never been paralleled. His idea was, that they should move in a perfect line, without either *opening, swerving, floating, doubling,* or *pressing*; that in every cadenced step, they should strike the ground, so as to make it resound, and, as it were, tremble and burn beneath their feet; nor is it possible to give any idea of it in any other words than his own:

οἱ δ᾽ ἄρ, ἴσαν, ὡσεί τε πυρὶ χθὼν πᾶσα νέμοιτο·
Γαῖα δ᾽ ὑπεςοναχιζε,

The vigour of this line is beyond the power of any translation. Although you cannot equal, it is laudable to imitate his precision in dressing and marching.

He prescribes no invariable order of battle; that must be adapted to the circumstances of place, time, &c. &c.

At one time you see him arranging his cavalry, that is, the chariots on the wings; these were perfectly dressed in three or more ranks, &c. according to their strength, and the nature of the ground, &c. The light armed troops, and the archers, &c. he adjusted generally in eight ranks, which composed the front. The heavy armed infantry composed his second line; this phalanx was a solid column, whose established order was sixteen deep. It was practised to take three kinds of order, viz. open, and two kinds of close order; the closest was termed constipation; it was precisely similar to that of his Majesty's forces, when the ranks are locked up and the elbows touch. The phalanx thus formed, levelled their pikes, which were fourteen cubits long, parallel to the horizon, and presented their left sides to the front in the charge. This position has been transmitted, and is equally practised by all the troops in Europe; the only difference is, that instead of pikes you level your firelocks, and instead of sixteen, you form in three ranks; instead of having your three ranks engaged, you can engage only one of them, whilst the remaining two, your centre and rear ranks, are idle, with arms ported.

The pikes of the front rank of the phalanx were thus protended ten cubits before it; the pikes of the second rank surpassed the front by eight cubits; those of the third by six; those of the fourth rank reached four cubits beyond the front; and the pikes of the fifth exceeded the front rank by two cubits. As in their closest order they had two men in their front, that is, double the number in the same space, more than any other troops, not similarly formed, could have; and as they could, from their construction, produce the five foremost ranks to the charge, consequently, their advantage in numbers was irresistible, being ten to one. As the eleven ranks which were adjusted behind the fifth rank, were in fact idle, and unable, from their situation, to partake in the charge, they were supposed to be of use in pressing upon the five foremost ranks. Although common sense might have pointed out that nothing could more impede the exertions of the front, than any pressure upon them from behind; and although the necessity of re-forming the idle ranks into such order as might give them an opportunity of co-operating, seems obvious, yet all attempts of this kind were long discountenanced, as being repugnant to established regulations, and the custom of the army. Such was Homer's construction of the phalanx, which was so greedily adopted by Epaminondas, Philip, &c. &c.

Upon another occasion you see him forming his chariots in the front, the light troops, and those he considered as the weakest, in the centre. The great bulwark of war, the heavy armed infantry, forms his third line.

This is the order of battle prescribed in the fourth book of his Iliad, and whatever you may think of it, it will be impossible for you to suppress your admiration of that great law which he lays down in regard to marching the forces. Have the goodness to peruse the thirteen lines beginning with the 297th, and ending with the 309th verse inclusive, of this book. The precept for marching with precision in the *line*, is not only laid before you, but enforced also by the highest rewards and punishments. Obedience to the law is beautifully enforced by punishment, in the following words :

"Ὃς δὲ κ' ἀνὴρ ἀπὸ ὧν ὀχέων ἕτερ' ἅρμαθ', ἵκηλαι
"Ἔγχει ὀρεξάσθω.

That is, whosoever shall go out of the line, repel him with your spear; literally, whatsoever man shall come from his own chariots to other chariots, extend the spear to aligne him. The passages preceding and subsequent to the above quotation, must be grateful to you in the elegant version of Mr. Pope :

1. *The Arrangement.*
" The horse and chariots to the front assign'd,
" The foot (the strength of war) he rang'd behind ;
" The middle space suspected troops supply,
" Inclos'd by both, nor left the pow'r to fly."

2. *The Dress in Line.*
" He gives command to curb the fiery steed,
" Nor cause confusion, nor the *ranks exceed*,
" Before the rest let none too rashly ride;
" No strength, nor skill, but *just in time*, be try'd :
" The charge once made, no warrior turn the rein,
" But *fight* or *fall* ; a firm embody'd train."——

3. *The Honors and Consequences of Obedience to these Laws.*
" Our great forefathers held this prudent course,
" Thus rul'd their ardour, thus preserv'd their force,
" By laws like these immortal conquests made,
" And earth's proud tyrants low in ashes laid."

F

It is evident, from every line in Homer, that if he had a fault, it consisted in his excess of accuracy in marching and dressing the forces square to the front. If a single man stood on parade, or marched, with any part of his face or shoulder half an inch out of the line, he considered the whole line deranged. The moderns have adopted his ideas as to dressing; but the officers having been once posted, he would permit no changing of their positions; he would not permit the Captain, for example, on the right to change to the left, and from that to the right, four times in the course of a few minutes.

Instructed by the precepts of Homer, Philip of Macedon reformed his phalanx, and subverted the liberties of Greece. This same discipline enabled Xenophon to perform wonders. This great, perhaps greatest of generals, and writers, took all his military ideas from Homer: with a mere handful, never exceeding 13,000 men, he surmounted every difficulty of rivers, mountains, and superior and surrounding enemies, and effected his famous retreat, after a march of 1155 leagues. Fired by these glorious exploits, and confident in the superiority of his military system, Philip projected the plan of overturning the Persian empire; fate prevented him from executing this project, which, of course, devolved upon his son. By the means of Homer, which he carefully placed under his pillow every night, Alexander readily accomplished what his father had so ably projected.

But, notwithstanding the invincible strength of the phalanx, yet this order had many imperfections; the individuals composing it could do nothing when separated; the objections to it did not escape the sagacity of Xenophon and Polybius.

Since the phalanx was impenetrable in front, &c. why was it defeated by the Romans? " Because," says Polybius, " in war, the times " and places of action are various and indefinite; there is, however, " but one time and place, one determinate mode of action suited to the " phalanx, which, if it obtain, it must be victorious. It requires a plain

" free from all obstructions of ditches, breaks, and obliquities, hills, rivers,
" &c. It is difficult to find twenty stadia in extent free from such ob-
" stacles; if such a space could be found, and the phalanx posted therein,
" the enemy, instead of approaching it, may readily direct their route
" through the country, take, and plunder the cities. If it relinquish
" its own proper ground and engage in action, the advantage is then
" much against it. Nothing is more easy than to avoid the places
" which are favourable to it; on the contrary, those that are unfa-
" vourable cannot be avoided; even in a plain, if attacked on the
" flanks and rear, it becomes disordered, and unable to defend itself
" without the operation of counter-marching the front to the rear,
" &c.; but this movement is too slow and dangerous in the crisis of
" action; the soldiers have not been instructed individually, and
" therefore when they become separated either in advancing or retreat-
" ing, they are easily defeated by men trained in the science of De-
" fence. On the contrary, the Roman soldier is instructed in the
" science of Defence; he is fitted equally for all times and places; he
" can equally exert his powers when separated from his platoon or
" company, as when he is united to it. The confusion or destruction
" of one or two maniples, or even cohorts, does not affect those re-
" maining. The movements of the Roman army are quick, short,
" and simple; those of the phalanx slow and complex; it cannot
" move 100 yards in a line without halting and dressing. The Roman
" order was equally adapted to marching and fighting; their rear was
" invincible; it consisted of the reserve, or triarii; this veteran body
" had only to face to the right about, and present the most formidable
" front to the enemy."

The Roman order of march was a formidable order of battle; they
generally marched *quadrato ordine,* that is, *in a square;* they had no
occasion for either *wheeling, filing,* or counter-marching, to form this
figure. Three sides of it were truly formidable: the rear, as has been
observed, was composed of the veterans, the triarii; the front, which

was not the most formidable side, was composed of the hastati ; the Principes composed the flanks, or right and left faces of the square, as is observed by Sallust, in his description of the march of Metellus, *transvorsis Principiis,* that is, the Principes in the flanks. The general had nothing to do but to halt his men, and to face them outwards, and they were in complete order to defend every side of the square, as in the case of Metellus, who was way-laid and surrounded by Jugurtha in the desarts of Numidia. You see, therefore, for the reasons collected from Polybius and others, that you had better simplify or give up a considerable part of the phalanx, and yet hold fast all the great military axioms of Homer, as they are applicable to all orders, and particularly calculated to inspire men with an enthusiasm to conquer, or die gloriously fighting for their country.

The military question which has been so much discussed from the days of Cyrus to this moment, relates to the best order of battle—what is the greatest number of ranks that can co-operate so as to produce the greatest effect by their united exertions in firing and in charging the enemy ? This question seems to have been decided by Xenophon above 2000 years ago.

The circumstance is found in the sixth book of his Cyropædia. On the day before the battle of Thymbra, Araspas having returned to Cyrus with the necessary information, as had been pre-concerted, stated, that the whole of Crœsus' forces, horse and foot, were formed thirty deep, excepting the Egyptians, whose invariable order was one hundred deep ; that they were drawn up in solid columns or squares; that the side of each square was one hundred ; that the Egyptians, notwithstanding their depth, occupied forty stadia in front ; that the plan was to encircle Cyrus, &c. The usual order of Cyrus was twenty-four deep, but the night before the battle, he ordered his forces to be drawn up the next morning in battle array only *twelve* deep, and to march and fight in this thin weak order. This sudden innovation excited fear and astonishment in the minds of all his veteran generals : prompted by their zeal for the honor of his Majesty's arms, one of

them in the name of all, represented his fears, that the sudden intro-
duction of this new order, which was so contrary to experience and the
rules so long established for the army, and particularly at such a moment, must eventually prove ruinous to his Majesty's service. Cyrus
replied, " that he considered that to be the best order, which would pro-
" duce the greatest number of men to act against the enemy. That
" any formation, which precluded more than one half of the forces from
" partaking of the glory of aiding their friends, and of destroying the
" enemy, must be radically vicious ; that the order of twenty-four deep
" was of that kind, and therefore he had changed it ; that he did not
" fear the enemy on account of their depth ; on the contrary, he only
" regretted that their formation was not 10,000 deep, for in that case,
" said he, you would have the fewer enemies to contend with."

Succeeding generals having been thus enlightened by Xenophon,
reflected whether the order of twelve deep, might not admit still further reduction. Accordingly, you see that in the process of time, this
order has been reduced to ten, to eight, to six, to five, to four, and
finally to the established order of three ranks. These are now arranged
like the three foremost ranks of the phalanx ; they are better armed,
as the firelock, armed with the bayonet, combines the properties of fire
and sword. Have the goodness to examine the Grecian formation
and evolutions, which are detailed in fifty-three sections by Claudius
Œlianus, and you will find the modern movements analogous to those
of the Greeks. The position, facings, and wheelings forward (they did
not wheel backward), are similar ; the mode of marching, counter-
marching, halting, and dressing square to the front ; the opening and
closing the ranks ; the marching in line, column, and echellon, and the
various changes of position, &c. &c. are similar to those now established by regulation. A modern translator has given two hundred
and eleven sections, on the science of military movements, but there
is not a single section for the purpose of instructing the battalion in the most essential of all essential requisites ; that is, in the
art of destroying the enemy in close action. By the movements the

men are brought to face the enemy; by dexterity in the manual, they can load and fire : the existing practice goes no further. Now, as the firelock is a hand weapon, as well as a missile, surely the powers of it as a lever, merit some little attention. Is it possible that any precision in marching square to the front, or dexterity in priming, loading and firing, or in fixing and unfixing bayonets, and in coming to the position which is prescribed for the charge, can give any idea of the use of the weapon ? Do you imagine that a rigid adherence to certain rules is necessary in the movements, and in the dexterous application of the hands, even in boxing; but that all rules and regulations for the defence of your existence with the hand weapon are idle and chimerical ? Risum teneatis !

This was not the opinion of his Majesty, when he most graciously condescended to approve the experiments exhibited before him : his Majesty did not think it consonant to justice, goodness, and wisdom, to plunge his brave soldiers into close action unprepared, before they had been instructed to make a single thrust or parade ; to require that they should play in concert, before they had learned the gamut. The royal approbation was founded in the most consummate wisdom.

In plate 12th, No. 1, you see the man standing erect, on a narrow base ; the firelock is not extended before him to defend or cover any part of his person ; on the contrary, it is interposed between him and the file, or the man on his right. He is not exercised to open his legs and sink down upon them in a martial attitude, to collect and direct his force ; he is ignorant of the art of making thrusts and parades ; he knows nothing of the use, and just mode of applying the wonderful powers of the weapon which is in his hands ; he has never heard of the *fort* and the *foible ;* this art is withheld, as if it were a secret of *Bona Dea,* or of the Eleusinian mysteries, too sacred to be revealed to his Majesty's subjects and soldiers. Thus you see the weak position of every man in the front rank, which is the only rank that can at this moment have any share in the charge. But are not the other two ranks present, and squared to the front, with arms ported, and ready

Plate XII.

R. Smirke jun. delin.

to supply the places of the men who may fall in the front? They are so, but the centre rank cannot partake in the charge; it could not reach the enemy, and much less could the third or rear rank, armed as it now is; therefore these two ranks carry their arms ported; besides, any efforts from the hinder ranks in aid of the front, could only impede the natural exertions of the front. You see then, that the front rank is the only one which can be engaged in close action, and that, in this most weak and preposterous position, and as unpractised in the powers of the lever, as the enemy with whom it may be committed.

If the writer is erroneous in his statement of facts, he will be thankful to any man who will take the trouble of shewing his errors by facts and experiments, which may be readily made with firelocks; these will produce intuition, which is the highest degree of knowledge.

Cyrus, with all due veneration for established customs, had no hesitation in giving the *truth* operation, although it was in direct opposition to the practice established. His Royal Highness the Commander in Chief, like Cyrus, who was the protector of science, has not only countenanced, but commanded the writer to lay open his thoughts freely upon this important subject. Now, after this cursory view of the high and dignified origin, and of the inherent radical defect of the established exercises, you are sufficiently prepared to resume the subject, and to apply the rigid principles of Defence in all circumstances of close action; and as the science of Defence seems to be the only remedy pointed out to supply this defect, you are requested to peruse the following section.

## SECT. VII.

*The Application of the Science of Defence to the Bayonet.*

WILL it not be difficult to instruct a battalion in the art of defending itself in close action ?   All arts appear to be either difficult or
easy, in proportion to our ignorance or knowledge of them.   If you
are practised in the three positions already described, and in the thrusts
and guards, all difficulty is surmounted; the same gamut which
enabled you to play on the violin, will serve you in learning to play on
the violincello.

This science will give you the advantage of two to one in all places
and times.   The two ranks, viz. the front and centre, may be consolidated into one in close action, and after that moment, resolved again
into two ranks.   Nothing can be more easy and simple than the mode
of performing these operations.   Thus, for example :—" Stand erect
" and squared to the front in the first position, like the soldier on
" parade, either with or without arms."   Practise without arms for a
few days.   As a centre rank man, " bring the ball of your left toe
" to your right heel, and spring on guard in your second position,
" your feet at right angles twenty-two inches asunder; advance your
" right foot eight or ten inches, and bring up the left eight or ten
" inches; continue thus to advance until you are halted."   There
can be no necessity (except for mere practice), to advance more than
three or four of these little paces, and to retire as many, beginning
your retreat with your left foot, always facing your adversary.   " Upon
" the word *halt*, stand fast; on the word *recover*, bring back your
" right foot to your left, spring about three inches to your left as you
" come to your first position square to the front.   As front rank man,
" keep your right foot fast, and throw back your left twenty-two

" inches, at right angles with your right on guard, in your second po-
" sition. Advance, and retire, as before. You will recover to your first
" position, by bringing up your left foot to your right : thus you will be
" fit to act, as either front or centre rank." The directions for one file
of the battalion will be intelligible to all :—a file, is a line of soldiers
justly arranged one behind the other.

### Directions for putting the Ranks on Guard.

" In rank and file, on the word on guard, you being a front rank man,
" throw back your left, and the centre rank man throws forward his right
" foot on your right, twenty-two inches, at the same instant ;" by these
means the centre rank becomes dressed, and consolidated in a line
with the front rank, in the strongest position, as in Plate 14th.

The mode of exercising the ranks is as follows :

| *Words.* | *Explanation.* |
|---|---|
| *Tow.* | The file, that is, the whole line, being now on guard, advances one step with the right foot eight or ten inches, and brings up the left eight or ten inches, so as to preserve the wide base. |
| *Tow.* | Do. any number of steps. |
| *Halt.* | They stand fast in the second position. |
| *Retire—Tow.* | The file moves back the left foot eight or ten inches, &c. and brings back the right an equal distance. |
| *Tow.* | Do. Do. until halted. |
| *Recover—Tow.* | The file, or battalion, recovers thus : the front rank by bringing *up* the left, and the *rear* rank by bringing *back* their right feet square to the front, in the first position. Practise thus in advancing, retiring, and allonging for five or six days without arms. You will easily throw yourself into the second position from the first, sixty times in a minute : when tired by this exercise, relax by marching. |

G

As the rear rank had been idle with arms ported, you face your men to the right about, and it becomes the front, and may be united and exercised with the centre rank as before. If your front rank is dressed in a line before it went on guard, it must also be so when on guard, as it holds the right foot fast on the line, and throws back the left. Habit will enable the centre rank to spring on guard in one motion, dressing with the front rank, and to recover also in one motion. It is obvious that the two ranks, the front and centre, may be as easily consolidated on guard with the left, as with the right in front, according to the practice of the phalanx. This body was not instructed to make thrusts and parades, and hence it was so easily conquered by the Romans, who were practised in the use of the hand weapon. The phalanx was justified in presenting the left side, as it was protected by the shield; but now, as you do not use shields, to present your left side thus unprotected, and to plunge it into close action without any idea of the fort or foible, seems to be an act of valour far surpassing the courage of Achilles, who refused to fight without his shield; however, you can have no occasion for the shield, for the use of the right hand in applying the *fort*, is termed dexterity. The right hand, whether from use or otherwise, is more dexterous than the left, and therefore there is some reason for giving it an opportunity of doing a duty congenial to it.

At the same time it must be extremely useful to practise with the left in front, as this will render the man ambidexter; but this science is equally necessary in either case.

In the present established position of the charge, the left side is presented as in No. 1, plate 12th. If you charge with the right in front, you will have a most decisive advantage, as appears from No. 2 of the same plate; for your firelock will be placed in the inside of his left arm, your *fort* applied to his *foible*, you stand upon a broad, while he stands upon a narrow base; you seize and bind down his foible by your right hand, your left holds the extremity of the butt of the piece, your right holds that part which is intermediate between the lock and the lowest pipe, your point is raised thirty-five degrees above the horizon, his point is parallel to the horizon, and if it be not, depress it with your *fort ;* by these means he must fall on your point, without any effort made on your part, as he is exposed from head to foot. Any effort of his to parry your point would be useless to him, and serve only as a fulcrum to your firelock. This is so evident, that had he the strength of fifty men in addition to his own, it would be impossible for him, in this situation, to guard himself; therefore the dexterity of your right hand applied in this manner, will answer all the purposes of a shield, perhaps as effectually as that of Achilles. As you have from this position, such facility to destroy your enemy, you may suppose, and with great justice, that any additional aid must be superfluous. Very true, you have one hundred to one in your favor.

But as the centre and rear ranks are idle, one of them may be employed in action, provided the men are not hunchbacked, or encumbered with knapsacks ; for the diameter of a man standing square to the front, taken from the extreme points of his shoulders, is double the line crossing that diameter at right angles; that is, the man occupies twice as much space by standing in his weak position square to the front, as when he stands in his strong martial position on guard; therefore at the instant the front rank comes on guard, the centre rank springs into the vacant intervals; thus, the two ranks are consolidated as in plate 12th, No. 2. In this situation the centre rank man has nothing to guard against, not even the *foible* of the enemy to oppose : he has only to destroy the enemy without any opposition. If this is the necessary result of your second position, what would the consequence be to the enemy, were you and your companion to make an exertion of your powers, that is, to allonge out in the third position ? You see that this practice gives two to one in the same space in the front, and that consequently it gives the same advantage in the *flanks* and rear, and *that,* in all times and places it must prove the inevitable destruction of the enemy. No line of troops can withstand your impulse for an instant in the field ; its utility is equally evident in the storming of fortresses, in the entering of breaches, and the cutting out of ships, &c. Twenty men disciplined in this manner, thrown on board of an enemy's ship, of whatever rate or force it may be, must be sure to carry her, by virtue of their having two to one in the same space, and above one hundred to one from the use of the powers of the lever; besides, this exercise must be equally useful in the repulse and destruction of any force attempting to board your ships; and it would give the marines such a decided advantage over the seamen, as would ensure good order and discipline, &c. Nothing can be more easy than to come from this, to the first position square to the front; the front rank has only to bring up its left foot, throwing up the piece to the shoulder at the same instant; or it may raise up its right hand with the firelock, and stand with arms ported, for the purpose of advancing to a second, third, or to more charges in succession. At the instant the front comes to the first position, the centre rank brings back the right foot to the left, which left foot has been moved three inches to the left in recovering; by this means the centre rank will dress and cover in one motion square to the front.

The following may be considered as a kind of lesson for this purpose.

The company or battalion being formed and told off, one half may be termed the right, the other the left wing; after opening the battalion from its centre, three or four paces by the side step, the wings may wheel inwards the quarter of the circle, and they will be confronted; any other mode of moving, so as to bring them opposite, will equally answer the purpose. When thus opposed, say, " prepare to charge," they come to the usual well known position. It is not material whether they prepare and charge with their right or left in front, the principle is the same, and they should be exercised in both methods.

| Words. | Explanation. |
|---|---|
| 1. *Prepare to charge.* | If the ranks are incorrect in coming to this position, explain and practise them by recovering, or reducing them into two ranks in the first position. It is impossible there should be any error if you have instructed them first, rank by rank, to take the positions separately. |
| *On guard.* | The front and centre are consolidated. The word applies to both wings. They join the barrels of their firelocks touching in a point, about twelve inches from the muzzles. The bayonets are not to be used for the first twelve days. |
| *The right wing will advance, and the left will retire.* | A caution to move step by step on any signal, such as the word *tow*, no fleugelman is necessary, as such cannot be used in real action. |
| *Tow.* | The right wing advances, and the left retires one step, according to the rule laid down for the advancing and retiring of a single man. |
| *Tow.* | Do. the wings proceed thus, until halted. |
| *Halt.* | They stand fast. |
| *The left wing will advance, &c.* | A caution that the left wing will advance, and the right will retire. |
| *Tow.* | The left wing advances one step, &c. and continues so to do, until halted. |
| *Halt.* | They stand fast. |
| *Recover.* | The front and centre rank of each wing, which when advancing on guard made one rank, are now reduced into two, dressed and covered square to the front. |
| *Prepare to charge.* | They come to the well known position. |

| Words. | Explanation. |
|---|---|

**On guard.**    The front and centre are united in one rank. An idea of this union may be conceived from plate 14th, which represents three files, or nine men; six of these, viz. the three men in the front, and the three in the centre rank, are consolidated in the second position on guard, whilst the rear rank is of course idle.

The objection to this plate is, that in it the men are not sunk low enough by six inches.

**The right wing will allonge, and the left will parry quarte. Tow.**    The man No. 1, plate 13th, represents the right wing allonging out in the third position, according to the rule laid down in section the 4th, for pushing quarte.

No. 2, of the same plate, represents one man, and consequently every man of the front rank of the left wing, in the proper attitude of parrying the thrust, with the *point volante*, as recommended in the 4th section.

**Tow.**    The left wing returns the thrust of quarte in the line, by applying the fort, and allonging together, and striking the ground with a sound and velocity like thunder. The right wing parries with the point volante.

**Tow.**    The right wing hurls down the thrust with the same velocity and precision. The wings alternately allonge and parry in this manner, during five or six minutes.

**Halt.**    They cease to allonge, and stand in the second position.

**Recover.**    They are reduced into three ranks, standing square to the front and shouldered.

Plate XIII.

Pointe Volante.

Allonge.

After practising thus, for four or five days, they are to be similarly exercised in disengaging and pushing, and parrying tierce, according to the rules laid down in section the 4th, for the thrust and guard of tierce.

Suffer them not to move or drag the hinder leg, which they would be apt to do, from their eagerness in the allonge. The firelock which appeared heavy to beginners, will, in the course of four weeks become so light, that they will readily hold it out with the one hand only, on the allonge. Observe, first to exercise them in the positions without arms; secondly, with the firelocks simply; and thirdly, you are to use the bayonet.

Lesson 2.—Suppose the battalion opposed, or not opposed to another battalion, " practise as follows:—1. Prepare to charge. 2. On guard, advance twice, and allonge in quarte. 3. Recover and parry quarte, with the point volante. 4. Return quarte. 5. Recover and parry quarte. 6. Disengage and push tierce. 7. Recover and parry tierce with the point volante. 8. Push tierce. 9. Recover and parry tierce." This practice continued for ten or twelve days, will give them such precision and vigor, that they will feel themselves confident, and justified in calling for the bayonet.

Perhaps the preceding lessons may be sufficient to enable men, not only to destroy any lines, one after the other, who would have the temerity to stand or come within reach, but to run also a considerable distance with celerity and order, and to pour destruction upon the enemy, however numerous their lines and reserves may be, one behind the other: however, the following is a lesson to which you may add *ad libitum*. 1. " Prepare to charge. 2. On guard. 3. Allonge in quarte. 4. Recover and parry quarte over with the round parade of quarte. 5. Circle twice, and push quarte over. 6. Recover with the point volante in tierce. 7. Cut vertically in tierce, and end this cut in a thrust. 8. Recover with the round parade twice made in tierce, and dart home in tierce. 9. Recover, using the round parade of tierce once, and come to the point volante in quarte. 10. Dart in a vertical cut in quarte, end it in thrust. 11. If he feigns or raises his point, time him on his first movement. 12. If he parries your quarte over, or tierce, as you recover, throw in the octave. 13. Retire, and if he advances in tierce, time him in quarte. 14. If he deceive your half circle, dart in the octave, &c. &c." However, simple quarte and tierce, and the guard of the point volante, will be very ample for soldiers.

---

## SECT. VIII.

### *Respecting the Mode of averting the Cuts of Cavalry.*

PERHAPS the equestrian art also proceeded from the East into Egypt, and thence into Greece. The Centaurs, a tribe of the Lapithæ, are said to have been the first who taught the horse to obey the rider. The ancient inhabitants of Thessaly being struck with the uncommon and formidable sight of a man mounted on horseback, concluded that it was a phenomenon of a monstrous animal composed of man and horse united.

Virgil, in his third Georgic, gives a beautiful description of this art, and its origin.

> " Primus Erichthonius currus, et quatuor ausus
> " Jungere equos, rapidisque rotis insistere victor.
> " Fræna Pelethronii Lapithæ, gyrosque dedere
> " Impositi dorso, atque equitem docuêre sub armis
> " Insultare solo, et gressus glomerare superbos."
>
> " Bold Erichthonius was the first who join'd
> " Four horses for the rapid race design'd ;
> " And o'er the dusty wheels presiding sate ;
> " The Lapithæ to chariots add the state
> " Of bits and bridles, taught the steed to bound,
> " To run the ring, and trace the mazy round ;
> " To stop, to fly, the rules of war to know ;
> " T' obey the rider, and to dare the foe."——DRYDEN.

Plate XIV.

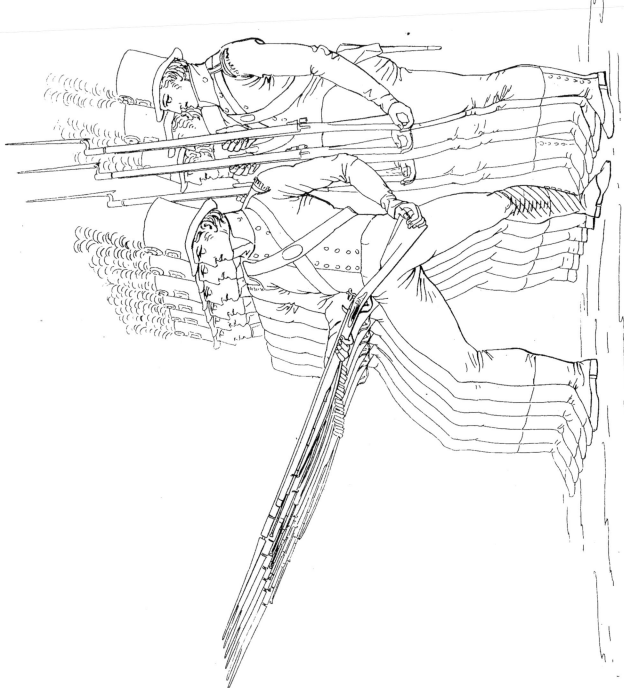

R. Inerke Jun. delin

Jn. de aqua

The superiority of the British Cavalry has been acknowledged, even by its most inveterate enemy; yet no body of cavalry could venture to rush upon an impenetrable chevaux de frise, and much less could they come within the reach of a body of infantry, supposed to be actually practised in the bayonet exercise. Nothing but temerity could urge them to make an experiment which must end in their destruction. See plate 14th. But it is out of the power of inanimate plates and words, to give any idea of the immense powers of men trained and invigorated to co-operate by means of this exercise.

You see that every cavalry man must have five bayonets to encounter, any one of which, in the hands of dexterity, must be sufficient to overpower him and his horse. The cavalry, in such circumstances, could only shew itself and feign to charge, and in common prudence wheel about in the expectation of an opportunity of meeting, or pursuing, some of the infantry which might be separated. Although men trained in this exercise, cannot be broken or separated in action, yet, let the possibility of such an event be admitted, for the purpose of indulging the cavalry man.

The cavalry man thinks that from his elevated situation, and his knowledge of the mode he has been taught of flourishng his sword, that he has an indubitable advantage. On the contrary, the infantry man who has been really instructed in the use of the sword, is convinced that the horseman does not, in truth, know how to make one single thrust or parade. An elevated situation is an advantage, if it can be used with effect. For this purpose, it is essential to have a broad and solid base to stand and move upon, freely and independently of the motions of another animal. The movements of the rider depend much on the situation and movements of his horse. He cannot with due celerity and quickness make the minute movements of one step, and of a step and a half, or of less than half a step, so as to be instantly within and without the proper distance at the same instant. The minute motions of the horse, are too slow and inaccurate for this purpose. The horse moves as he may be commanded; his ear and

H

reason are centered in his mouth, which is governed by the bit; this by the reins, and these are directed by the rider. On the contrary, the infantry man, although inferior in situation, stands ready, collected, and independent upon a broad base, upon terrâ firmâ; he knows and takes his distance at a glance; he is trained in the method of anticipating his enemy; he *nicks* the critical moment, and delivers the *time thrust*, to which the horseman is a stranger. In delivering this thrust, he knows and applies the fort of his firelock, which is a formidable weapon, to the *foible* of the sword, which is a trifling, insignificant weapon, in comparison with the bayonet.

In plates 15th and 16th, the cavalry man is placed in the most favourable position for cutting and thrusting, and the infantry man in the most disadvantageous situation that could be selected, viz. on the off-side. He has nothing to do but to form his *extension*, raising his hands and arms in the line about two inches above his forehead; he is thus completely shielded, and ready to dart the time thrust into the cavity under the arm. It is manifest that the horse is exposed also in every part that comes within the reach of the bayonet, and that a slight prick in the flank is incurable. As the horseman uses his right, so the infantry man presents his left in front. It is also to be seen, that were the infantry man to exert his powers, that is, to allonge, the destruction of the cavalry man must be inevitable.

The charge against the infantry man must be either in a perpendicular, or in an oblique direction. If the horse is stimulated forward for the purpose of prostrating the infantry man by the collision of the horse against him, the impetuosity exerted in the perpendicular, will answer no purpose, but to ensure the destruction of the innocent animal; for in this case, the horse is forced to rush upon the point which will be projected by all the powers of the infantry man, and the force of the impulse will be doubled, on account of the force and velocity of the horse. The horse, therefore, will be destroyed, and that too, unprotected by the rider. For no horseman, however dexterous as a swordsman, will be able, from his situation in the saddle, to parry

Plate XV.

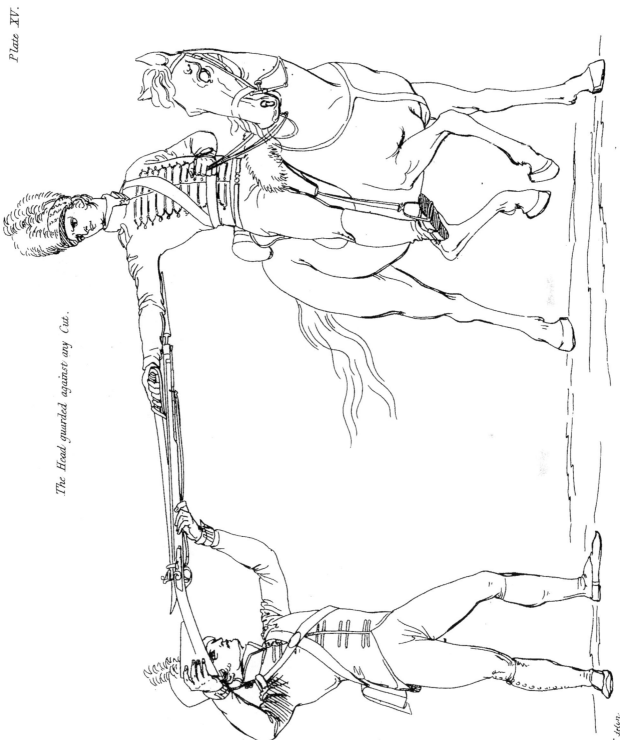

The Head guarded against any Cut.

Plate XVI.

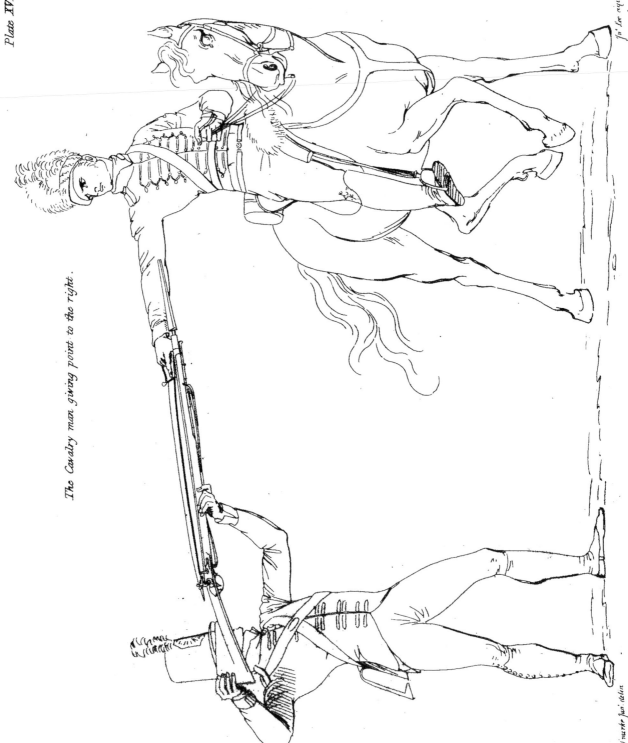

The Cavalry man giving point to the right.

Plate XVII.

The situation of the Cavalry man on the Near Side.

Plate XVIII.

The cut of the Cavalry.

R. Smirke Jun. delin.

Jn.º Lee aqua.

any impulse of the bayonet directed in a right line against the face, nose, and eyes of his horse; his inclination forward will not accomplish it. He will not, therefore, venture to sacrifice his horse, and perhaps himself, by an enterprise of this kind, but rather check and wheel his horse to his left, for the purpose of obtaining the advantage of having the infantry man as before, on the *off-side*. For nothing can be more evident, than that his only chance of saving himself and the horse depends upon this circumstance.

Suppose that the horseman were for a moment to neglect this precaution, and to suffer his left or near side to be exposed. The destruction of the horse and his rider must be the consequence, as in plate 17th. The situation and the weakness of the guards of *prime*, *quinte*, and the guards termed *protects*, concur in effecting this purpose. These kind of parades can be hazarded against such infantry only, as are not exercised in applying the principles of the science of Defence; the present is a different case, the infantry man is supposed here to be completely practised. As the infantry man is trained to defend himself in all possible situations, so the cavalry man can make no defence except in one solitary position, to obtain which he will make every effort. Suppose that he has now succeeded, and, confident in his strength, prepares to make a forcible cut against the infantry man, plate 18th. On his first movement into this position, the infantry man anticipates him, by simply forming his extension, and by infixing the point into the side exposed: this is executed with such celerity, that the wound is inflicted before the thrust can be seen or guarded. Such must be the inevitable consequence of a conflict in close action with a real swordsman, critically conversant in the bayonet exercise; his parades are thrusts, and all his thrusts are destruction to the aggressor.

More, much more, could-be said and written upon every part of this important subject. Confident that what has been offered will be honored with due attention, the Writer hastens to the conclusion. If he has failed in the explanation of the principles of his System of Defence, and of its decisive advantages against either infantry or cavalry : if he has not fully obeyed the orders of His R. H. the Commander in Chief, that failure will be imputed to the true cause—to the want of strength and perspicuity in the Writer, and not to any weakness in the principles of the Science, which are eternal and immutable. His gratitude and feelings for the honor conferred upon this occasion, can be more easily conceived than expressed.

" Ille<br>
" Ludere quæ vellem calamo permisit agresti."

With the most profound respect, therefore, he lays this mite of assistance, for the public service, at the feet of His Royal Highness, and the Public.

ANTHONY GORDON,

A. M. T. C. D.

# APPENDIX.

———

*Letter from the late General Burgoyne, to General Sir William Pitt, (at that time Commander in Chief of the Forces in Ireland.)*

[General Burgoyne has been, and ever will be, known and venerated by the public, on acount of his immortal productions. The force, beauty, and elegance of his compositions, had united the suffrages of the public in his favour, even during his life time. He did not rest satisfied with a superficial smattering, but penetrated into the deepest recesses of Science. He was universally respected by all who were not strangers to his virtues, as the bright ornament, not only of the military, but of humanity. But his elegant accomplishments—his erudition, which was profound, various, and extensive, were nothing when compared to the unbounded goodness of his heart, and the strength of his friendship. He was a father to the fatherless and benefactor to the pennyless. His greatest delight and study, consisted in devising means for the encouragement of such as he thought worthy of it. The following is selected as one instance, from the many which might be produced, to shew the magnanimity of the General, struggling to support an insignificant Subaltern, who, in his opinion, was labouring in the cause of truth.]

———

*Bath, November 20th,* 1787.

MY DEAR GENERAL,

      I had designed a letter for you to Dublin before I came to Bath, but I heard you were on the point of embarking for England: I then left it in London, to be delivered at your arrival; and circumstances being since altered by the accession of a new Administration in Ireland, I have recalled that former letter, and take up my pen anew.

The reason of thus troubling you, proceeds from a sincere concern for the disappointment of Lieut. Gordon, of the 67th regiment. You know my thoughts of his zeal, his activity, his depth of military theory, and his merit in having reduced it to practice in his bayonet exercise : but he has testimonies of far greater consequence in his favour, viz. your commendation and very honorable protection ; the same from the Duke of Rutland, marked in the strongest manner by word of mouth, and by recommendation to the King ; and lastly, a message from His Majesty, after he had seen the experiment, by the Adjutant General, expressing his Royal and high Approbation. The King at the same time ordered a sum of money for Mr. Gordon, as a reimbursement of his expences, in training and marching his men, and other contingencies ; in that light only he received it ; in fact, it did not more than reimburse him, and I know he would humbly have de-livered it, had it been understood as a reward of his pains. His spirit suggested, that if his attempt at an improvement in the Service had been judged unworthy notice, it would have been his part to have bowed to that decision : but that countenanced and recommended by Commanders in Chief, and a Lord Lieutenant, and finally stampt with the Royal Opinion in its favour, he might look without arrogance to the only true reward of his profession, the honor of employment, and the prospect of rank.

In regard to his exercise, it is admitted by the very few who have seen and understood it, that it gives uncommon vigor, dexterity, and confidence to the men conversant in it ; that it actually doubles the number of the forces in the crisis of action, by his ingenious mode of introducing the centre rank into the front, and by placing them in the strongest attitude to act together in offence and defence. This is a wonderful addition of strength, and not attended with any addition of expence ; it requires only labour and attention.

Yet Lieut. Gordon has had the misfortune to remain unnoticed from the time he was approved. I would be very sorry that his feelings, which are very acute, should urge him to quit the Service ; I sincerely think he would be a great loss to it.

The prejudice of party, of attachment to old practices, and preconceived contempt of innovation, but above all, the want of a Commander in Chief, render it impossible at present to revive the matter on this side the water. I have advised Mr. Gordon to make a new and more concise statement of his system, and convinced as I am from the experiments I have witnessed, of the solid principles upon which it is built, I shall very readily annex the remarks which occurred to me when I first espoused it.

This paper I shall advise him, with your concurrence, to lay before the Marquis of Buckingham, who will give it, I am sure, due attention. I would then submit to you, my dear Sir, what, had I been in a situation of power and favour, I should have proposed myself, the drilling the Dublin Garrison, or such part of it as you may chuse, under his inspection in the bayonet exercise, for the purpose of the Lord Lieutenant's being a judge at the spring reviews, and the knowledge of it becoming more extended.

His misfortune is, that Officers have formed judgments upon hearsay or cursory thoughts.

Upon sight, it would carry mathematical demonstration, and Lord Buckingham is a man that, if convinced, would renew and support it. If not convinced, the regiments would only have had the very small labour of additional exercise of legs and arms, which considered abstractedly must be of benefit.

I expect you will find some degree of coldness or slight among parts of any garrison, to an attempt of this nature, but I know that will not prevent your countenance, if you think an essential improvement in the Service, or the protection of a worthy Officer is in question.

I shall be happy to receive your sentiments.

Dear Sir,

Most faithfully yours,

J. BURGOYNE.

*General Pitt,*
*Commander in Chief of the Forces in Ireland,*
*&c. &c. &c.*

*Sketch of the Bones and Muscles of the Arm, and of its Powers as a Lever, &c.*

As the system of Defence proposed by Gordon, is an innovation, opposite in many respects to the French practice, it is a duty incumbent upon him, to shew that his principles are conformable to those of nature, of anatomy, and the powers of the lever, to all which the established principles are diametrically repugnant.

He will not enter into any minute detail of the figure, position, and functions of the bones and muscles of the arm; such would be indispensable for medical purposes only; his attempt will be confined. Some general idea of the arm is necessary to ascertain its motions and powers, and the best mode of applying these to advantage in the science of Defence.

The whole hand or arm, from the collar bone inclusive, to the ends of the fingers, is composed of thirty-two bones. That long bone which is between the shoulder blade bone and the elbow, is properly called the arm, *(os humeri)*. It is a lever of the third kind; for its fulcrum or prop, is the cavity of the shoulder blade bone; its moving powers are the seven muscles, which are appropriated and inserted into it, for the purpose of raising, extending, turning, &c. &c. it, in all directions upon its base, which is the cavity already mentioned.

The lower end of the arm is broader, and opens into cavities for the reception of the processes of the fore-arm.

The two bones called the ulna and radius, constitute the fore-arm, which reaches from the elbow to the wrist.

The ulna is on the outside of the radius, in a line with the little finger. The radius is situated on the inside of the fore-arm, in a line with the thumb. The ulna and radius are firmly cemented together at both ends. The ulna furnishes the socket for that purpose at the upper end, and the radius gives the socket to the ulna at the lower end of the fore-arm. These two bones, that is, the fore-arm, is a lever of the third kind, whose base or prop is the lower end of the arm, viz. the *pulley* or pivot, upon which the fore-arm is moved, and the moving powers are the muscles, which are termed, from their uses, flexors and extensors, and the pronators and supinators.

The wrist is composed of eight bones, compacted in a double row, and articulated to the lower extremity of the fore-arm, upon which, as a base, the wrist performs all the motions peculiar to itself.

The metacarpus consists of five bones connected with the wrist. The metacarpus serves as a base on which the thumb and fingers are moved. The thumb is composed of two, and each of the fingers of three bones, which from their articulation in close order, are termed phalanges.

A muscle is a fibrous fleshy substance, the immediate organ of motion. All the functions of the different members, &c. are performed by the muscles. Muscular motion is either voluntary, involuntary, or mixed.

The voluntary motions result from the commands of the mind, wonderfully but unaccountably impressed on the muscles by the nerves, who are the ministers for the purpose of thus communicating orders from within, outwards, or for carrying intelligence from without, inwards, for the information of the mind. Although the exertion of all the muscles is indispensable in Defence, and although they merit a minute detail and attention to their origin, uses, and insertion, yet, the Writer will content himself with giving only a hasty sketch of the pronators and supinators, as these are appropriated to the rotation of the fore-arm, wrist and hand, in the execution of all cuts, thrusts, and guards. The present doctrine is, that all cuts, thrusts, and guards are made by the action of the wrist and shoulder *alone*. They say, " that to make a cut with effect, and at the same time without exposing " the person, there are two points which principally demand attention. " The first is, to acquire a facility in giving motion to the arm, by

I

58

" means of the wrist and shoulder, without bending the elbow; for
" in bending the elbow, the sword-arm is exposed; a circumstance of
" which the opponent will ever be ready to take his advantage; as a
" cut in that quarter may be made with the greatest security, and if
" it be well directed, with the most fatal effect, as it at once decides
" the issue of the contest. Above all, take care never to bend the el-
" bow, &c. The action of the wrist and shoulder alone direct the
" blade, &c. independent of the motion of the arm."

" Again, all parades, such as *quarte, tierce,* &c. &c. are to be made
" by the mere motion of the wrist alone, independent of any motion of
" the arm, &c.

These errors are widely diffused. A practice conformable to such
fundamental principles, will subject you to every cut and thrust delivered by a real swordsman: it is repugnant to muscular motion, as
may appear from the following table.

The first column contains the names; the second, the head and
origin; the third, the points of insertion; and the fourth column
specifies the uses of the muscles, appropriated to pronation and supination.

## The Pronator Muscles.

| Names. | Origin whence. | Insertion into. | Use of, &c. |
|---|---|---|---|
| 1. Pronator radii teres. | The internal condyle of os humeri, and the edge or coronoid process of the ulna. | The middle of the outer part of the radius. | To roll the radius, the wrist and the palm inwards, all together at the same instant. |
| 2. Pronator radii quadratus. | The inner and lower part of the ulna. | The lower part of the radius opposite to its origin. | To turn the radius in common with the wrist and hand prone downwards and inwards. |
| 3. Flexor carpi radialis. | The internal condyle of the humerus. | The metacarpal bone of the fore finger, which sustains that finger. | To bend the hand and to assist the preceding muscles in turning the hand with the wrist and fore-arm into pronation. |

Hence it is impossible to turn the wrist or the hand into pronation independent of the radius or fore-arm: they move together; the arm must be moved in that direction with the wrist.

## The Supinator Muscles.

| Names. | Origin whence. | Insertion into. | Use of, &c. |
|---|---|---|---|
| 1. Supinator radii longus. | The external condyle of the humerus. | The radius, near the styloid process. | To roll the radius outwards, and with it the wrist and palm upwards, at the same time. |
| 2. Supinator radii brevis. | The outer condyle of the humerus, and the upper edge of the ulna. | The head, the inner and upper part of radius, &c. | To roll the radius outwards, and to assist the anconeus, and to turn the hand-wrist, &c. up supine. |
| 3. The biceps flexor cubiti. | Two heads, one from the coracoid process, the other called the long head, from the upper edge of the glenoid cavity of the scapula. | The tubercle on the upper end of the radius, by a strong round tendon, &c. | To bend the arm with force, and to aid the wrist and the hand in turning upwards into supination or quarte. |

From the preceding table, of the origin, insertion, and uses of these muscles, it is manifest that the wrist cannot be moved into pronation and supination, or into the guards of quarte and tierce, by its own mere motion alone, independent of the motion of the fore-arm. On the contrary, it is impossible for any man to move his wrist into these positions, without moving his fore-arm at the same time, in the same direction. Try it by experiment: thus, hold the radius and ulna, or your right fore-arm, with your left hand, and move your wrist into supination and pronation, or into quarte and tierce. If you can turn your wrist into these directions, without turning the bones of your fore-arm at the same moment; in that case, the French are clearly right in their doctrine.

Besides, it is held as a maxim, that the arm is to be extended for its preservation. The extension of the arm, so far from protecting, exposes it to every cut, and that too, without any power of guarding itself. It is clear that the arm moves and defends itself by the powers of its muscles; the powers of the muscles are already exerted to the utmost in the position of extension. In that position they can make no further exertion. To make any effort of defence or offence, the muscles must be contracted; that is, the arm must be bent at the elbow. If the extension alone constitutes the safety of the arm, it will remain long unguarded. No, no, there is a particular mode of defending the arm, that is not extension; any of the round parades will shield the arm, and not one single parade can be made safely with an extended arm. The arm is to be invariably bent more or less at the elbow, and reserved for the purpose of being extended in delivering home the cut or thrust, after which it is to be instantaneously contracted to repeat the effort; besides, no man can hold his sword with an extended arm six minutes without pain.

*A Sketch of the Lever of the Third Kind.*

THE stab given to Archimedes, at the moment his divine faculties were intent upon the invention and demonstration of a mathematical theorem, was inflicted by an illiterate barbarian. Science has regretted, and ever will sympathize with Marcellus, in deploring a mortal wound inflicted on the father of Science, and more especially of the mechanic powers. There are six simple mechanic powers, from the combination of which the most complicated machines are constructed.

The principal of the six, is the lever, which is of three kinds, by reason of the different situation of the fulcrum or prop, in respect to the moving power and the weight.

In the first, the prop is between the power and the weight, and the nearer it is to the weight the more powerful is this lever.

In this lever, and universally, the power and the weight will be in equilibrio, that is, will balance each other, when they are reciprocally proportional to their distances from the prop.

In the second kind, the weight is between the prop and moving power, as a sedan chair, carried by two chairmen; doors moving on hinges, &c.

In the third kind, the moving power is between the prop and the weight, and generally placed nearer to the prop or centre of motion, and in some instances so near as to be almost identical. Therefore this kind of lever is the most disadvantageous, and more particularly when the weight is great and unhandy; as in the instance of a ladder to be raised up against a wall. But for the ordinary purposes of life, it is the most quick and commodious. Hence, and on account of the beauty and symmetry of the parts, the ALMIGHTY, in his infinite wisdom, was graciously pleased to form the legs and arms of animals levers of the third, rather than of the first or second kind.

Now, as the legs and arms are thus divinely composed, and as all instruments, such as swords, firelocks, pikes, sticks, &c. &c. are levers of this kind, and whereas there is a great *waste* of the muscular powers, insomuch, that not one sixtieth part of the power of one muscle is actually used and applied, but on the contrary, it is either lost or misapplied, as is observed and proved by Doctor Monro : perhaps you may consider an attempt to collect, concentrate, and mechanically to apply, if *not the whole*, yet certainly a considerable portion of these powers in a favourable light.

Reader, your attention is requested for about three minutes longer to this subject, and particularly to an observation of Mr. Gibbon, and of other luminous writers, on the power of discipline. They observe, that when a certain number are disciplined, their advantage over men utterly undisciplined, is as 100 to 1. Take an individual soldier, however practised he may be in the movements, the manual, and platoon exercise, and let him be committed in single combat with a sailor, or with a rustic not disciplined in these exercises, will he retain the superiority of 100 to 1, in his favor? No, so far from it, that the benefit of his discipline is scarcely perceptible, and victory may incline to the side of the sailor. Nevertheless, the advantage of discipline, which is imperceptible in the individual, increases in proportion to the number disciplined, and becomes as 100 to 1, in any considerable body of men instructed to act together.

Now, it is not the mere assertion of an individual, but an incontrovertible fact, repeatedly proved by experiments, that the System of Defence submitted to you, invigorates every man conversant in it, and armed with a firelock, with an addition of power greater than his former power, in the proportion of 60 to 1. Observe also, that it incontrovertibly doubles the number of the forces thus invigorated, by the simple and easy mode of introducing the centre rank, and consolidating it with the front, in the crisis of action, in all times and places ; therefore it gives an immediate individual advantage of 120 to 1, over every individual of the enemy. This, however, is the advantage that a small division, not exceeding forty-eight or fifty men, must have ; and, according to the observation of Mr. Gibbon, this power will increase in proportion to the number of men who may be instructed to co-operate; for men trained in this exercise must act against all other men not trained, as disciplined men against men utterly undisciplined in it. What the effect of such an immense accumulation of power must be, in an army of forty or fifty thousand men thus instructed, is with deference left to your calculation, for it is beyond the reach of the Writer.

" But you have not shewn the practicability of giving a single indi-
" vidual a power sixty times greater than his former power, and there-
" fore your conclusions fall to the ground." Answer, this fact is more easily demonstrated by experiments than by words. These have been exhibited, and may be repeated.

The demonstration, however, shall be attempted even in words, for your satisfaction.

It has been premised, that the whole arm, which is composed of thirty-two bones, is a compound lever of the third kind; that the lower end of the os humeri is the base or prop of the fore-arm ; that upon this base all the motions of the flexion, extension, supination, and the pronation of the fore-arm are performed ; and that on the same base also are performed all the motions of the supination and pronation of the wrist, in common with and not independent of the fore-arm.

The moving powers of the fore-arm are the muscles, already mentioned. Take a firelock or any other weapon in your hand or hands ; this weapon, held by your hands, becomes a lever of the same description. If you desire to know precisely the powers of this weapon for the purpose of using them against the enemy, they will be found thus : Resolve the compound lever into its simple constituent parts, that is, find out by experiments the different powers of all the different points of the simple lever. The powers of the simple lever being thus found, will most precisely give and determine the different powers of every point or hair's breadth of the compound lever; and the powers of every point of the lever, whether simple or compound, are in the reciprocal proportion of their distance from the fulcrum or prop (which prop, in the Science of Defence, is termed the fort), that is, the power of any point of the firelock (for example) increases in proportion as its distance from the fort diminishes, and the power gradually becomes less and less, as the distance from the fort increases.

*Demonstration.*—Take that part of the whole arm, called the fore-arm, which extends from the elbow to the ends of the fingers; consider it as a simple lever; divide it into any number of aliquot parts, that is, parts commensurate to it, say into 20. Apply 20 lbs. to the elbow, and 1 lb. to the fingers of the fore-arm extended parallel to the horizon, and these weights will be equal. The powers of the fore-arm, that is, the powers of the simple lever, being thus determined, necessarily determine the powers of the compound. For as the power of the elbow is to that of the fingers (20 :: 1 :), so is the power of the fort of the firelock (the fort is the part held by the hand), to that point of it which is distant a cubit from the fort, in the same proportion (20 :: 1 :). The power of the fort is to the power of the point at double that distance as 40 to 1, and it is to triple, quadruple, and quintuple that distance, as 60 to 1, as 80 to 1, and as 100 to 1 respectively; therefore the power of the fort of the firelock, which is held by both hands, is above 100 times greater than the power of the foible. Therefore any person conversant in these powers, that is, in applying the fort to the foible, has the advantage of 100 to 1. But 60 is less than 100, being but a part of it. It is manifest, therefore, that he may have 60 to 1 in his favour, in all times and places of close action whatsoever.

Quod erat demonstrandum.

But His Majesty's brave soldiers have neither time nor capacity to spare, in the culture of a laborious exercise, founded upon the principles of anatomy and those of mechanic powers.

It is impossible to become eminent in any art without some labor and attention; but if half the time, which is so meritoriously devoted to the movements and the manual, were bestowed upon the Science of Defence, the soldier, in that time, would not only be rendered more firm and correct in all the movements, but more confident from his knowledge of the Art of Defence; for there is an intimate and natural connexion between the arts; they conspire to aid each other. The Science of Defence diffuses a particular grace and energy over all the sister exercises, and facilitates the acquisition of them.

If it be true that a soldier cannot be too much exercised, as he has much time, some small daily portion of it might be thus beneficially occupied.

As to the theory of mechanics, it cannot be necessary to the soldier. The man who conducts the waggon, regards not the theory of the wheel and axle.

Thus soldiers might be instructed to apply the fort to the foible, and to demonstrate the truth by their practice, although strangers to the mathematical principles.

Gordon would be happy to testify his respect and gratitude to the many Noblemen and Gentlemen who have honored his System of Exercise with their approbation, if he could enumerate their highly respectable names. Among these illustrious personages, he considers himself psrticularly indebted to General Sir William Pitt, the Marquis of Buckingham, the late Sir William Fawcett, and Sir Adam Williamson.

The Generals declared publicly, " that what they had seen was " wonderful and incredible; that the adoption of it must advance the " King's troops in discipline two hundred years before any others; " that they never could have believed in the truth of the system had " they not been witnesses of it."

K

Gordon is equally obliged to the Earl of Buckinghamshire, and to Captain Merry, who commands the Gentlemen of the War-office. Captain Merry being an eminent swordsman, soon penetrated into the bottom of the subject. Major-General Calvert, the Adjutant-General, has honored the Science in very flattering terms; he has been pleased to ask, why a system so self-evident had not been adopted? There are many other illustrious characters, and one in particular, whose friendship and protection have been an ornament to Gordon for these last twenty years. He adorns the list of Major Generals; his greatest delight consists in doing good, and in concealing the glory of it. To this singular character Gordon owes every thing that he possesses, and yet he is not at liberty to gratify himself by naming him. There is another noble character, his very able and worthy friend Colonel Philip Robinson, distinguished for his depth of military science, who has been an advocate for instructing men in the art of defending themselves, for these twenty years past. He and Captain Merry disciplined the War-office Company; he gave his very able assistance also in drilling the Detachment of the Foot Guards.

" O happy Friends! sure, if my word could give
" Immortal life, your Fame should ever live."

**THE END.**